TALKING
ABOUT
BPD

of related interest

The Reality of Recovery in Personality Disorder
Heather Castillo
ISBN 978 1 84905 605 2
eISBN 978 1 78450 071 9

Hell Yeah Self-Care!
A Trauma-Informed Workbook
Alex Iantaffi and Meg-John Barker
ISBN 978 1 78775 245 0
eISBN 978 1 78775 246 7

What I Do to Get Through
How to Run, Swim, Cycle, Sew, or Sing Your Way Through Depression
Edited by Olivia Sagan and James Withey
Foreword by Cathy Rentzenbrink
ISBN 978 1 78775 298 6
eISBN 978 1 78775 299 3

Unlock Your Resilience
Strategies for Dealing with Life's Challenges
Stephanie Azri
Foreword by Rachel Kelly
ISBN 978 1 78775 102 6
eISBN 978 1 78775 103 3

We're All Mad Here
The No-Nonsense Guide to Living with Social Anxiety
Claire Eastham
Foreword by Natasha Devon MBE
ISBN 978 1 78592 082 0
eISBN 978 1 78450 343 7

Living at the Speed of Light
Navigating Life with Bipolar Disorder, from Depression
to Mania and Everything in Between
Katie Conibear
Foreword by Calum Harris, Lorraine Gillies and Aditya Sharma, National
Specialist Adolescent Mood Disorders Service, CNTW NHS Foundation Trust
ISBN 978 1 78775 557 4
eISBN 978 1 78775 558 1

Talking About BPD

A Stigma-Free Guide to Living a Calmer, Happier Life with Borderline Personality Disorder

Rosie Cappuccino

Foreword by Kimberley Wilson

Jessica Kingsley Publishers
London and Philadelphia

First published in Great Britain in 2022 by Jessica Kingsley Publishers
An Hachette Company

1

A CIP catalogue record for this title is available from the
British Library and the Library of Congress

ISBN 978 1 78775 825 4
eISBN 978 1 78775 826 1

Printed and bound in Great Britain by TJ Books Limited

Jessica Kingsley Publishers' policy is to use papers that are natural,
renewable and recyclable products and made from wood grown
in sustainable forests. The logging and manufacturing processes
are expected to conform to the environmental regulations
of the country of origin.

Jessica Kingsley Publishers
Carmelite House
50 Victoria Embankment
London EC4Y 0DZ

www.jkp.com

To every person with a diagnosis of borderline personality disorder or who relates to this diagnosis. If you relate to the fear, shame and loneliness described in this book, I hope it brings you validation, comfort and confidence.

Contents

Disclaimer

This book is not intended as medical advice. It is not a substitute for professional help. It is not written by a doctor, but by a person with lived experience. Always ask a doctor for medical advice and seek emergency help if in immediate danger.

Trigger warning
This book mentions abuse (emotional abuse, verbal abuse, child abuse, child neglect, abusive relationships and toxic relationships), anxiety and panic attacks, depression, dissociation, intrusive thoughts, self-harm, suicide (suicidal ideation and suicidal thoughts) and trauma (post-traumatic stress disorder, PTSD).

The following are also mentioned in passing: abuse (physical abuse, absent parent), alcohol, anger issues, bipolar disorder, blood, bullying, death, depersonalization disorder, drugs, eating disorder, hallucinations and delusions, homophobia and hate crimes, hospitalization, manipulation, misogyny, obsessive-compulsive disorder (OCD), rape and sexual assault, schizophrenia and transphobia.

Foreword

We should not tell people that it's 'good to talk' about a mental health condition without actively ensuring that the environment is one in which it is safe for them to do so. Too often for people with a diagnosis of borderline personality disorder (BPD) the social environment is not one that is conducive to them being open about their diagnosis; such a disclosure is still too often met with out-dated stereotypes and harmful caricatures.

I met Rosie when she generously agreed to be a guest on my podcast as part of a series I recorded on BPD. Having trained in dialectical behaviour therapy (DBT) early in my career, I wanted to lend my voice to creating a more thoughtful and compassionate public conversation about what it means to have BPD. During the discussion Rosie described experiences of discrimination from both friends and professionals that will be familiar to many people facing this diagnosis.

Dehumanizing judgements from the outside world don't just make disclosing BPD fraught with difficulty and risk; they can also undermine a person's internal experience. On a hot summer's day, a new client explained that they felt anxious about telling me that they were feeling uncomfortably warm in my consulting room because, "It's manipulative of me to say that I am hot because then that puts pressure on you to turn the air conditioning on." Comments and beliefs like these highlight how the general portrayal of BPD is so toxic that simply asking for basic needs to be met can leave people wondering whether they are causing harm. It is deeply saddening to be confronted with someone who has internalized the stereotypes of this diagnosis. Their hurt is palpable. As is the loneliness of being so negatively characterized and misunderstood. I hope we can all agree that anyone facing a mental health diagnosis deserves better than this.

So, are things getting better? Well, as is so often the case, it's a mixed picture. On the one hand, social media has enabled and empowered those with lived experience of BPD to share their own stories, build supportive communities and challenge the dominant illness narratives. However, it is true that there are, sadly, still some professionals who hold and perpetuate stigmatizing views and, as uncomfortable as this is to acknowledge, it is important that we do not turn a blind eye to this reality. To do so would be a disservice to the profession and the people we are trying to support. It is crucial that mental health professionals are deliberate in working to undo the stigmatized (and often misogynistic) representations of BPD, and it is for this reason that I hope professionals, as well as individuals with BPD and their friends and family, read this book. Yes, as health professionals we are human, and as humans we are susceptible to holding, perpetuating or failing to challenge biases that might negatively affect those we work with. However, as health professionals we have an ethical responsibility to seek out and address these biases so that we may offer the best care possible. As some of Rosie's own examples (see Chapter 4) attest, a careless, off-hand comment from a health professional can create lasting wounds. Whilst none of us can ever be perfect, I believe we should all aim to be better.

And we get better by listening. Too often we are keen to speak on behalf of those with a diagnosis without making space for their voices, without really listening. But the positive and accurate representation of people with a BPD diagnosis is important for all of us: patients, public, professionals.

For those with a diagnosis of BPD, this book is a comprehensive and compassionate resource to help make sense of their experiences. Rosie provides a framework for understanding some of the most distressing experiences and behaviours associated with BPD and valuable coping tools, and provides a hopeful example that these ways of being can be shifted and the underlying emotional needs understood and met. She challenges the perception that life with BPD is bleak or impossible. Rosie brings a gentle authority to the book, like a thoughtful and kind friend who, having been through it already, is on hand to help guide you through what can be a confusing and isolating experience.

That said, I sincerely hope that at least some of you are the friends, relatives, partners or colleagues of people with BPD, as well as health professionals, because solipsistic well-being is an illusion. The reality is that good mental health is a community endeavour. We cannot say 'it's good to talk' without being truly committed to listening. Hearing people with this diagnosis speak for themselves helps us to see the person and not the diagnosis. It is deeply humanizing, which in itself is a step towards healing.

And that is why this book makes me hopeful. Hopeful that individuals who receive this diagnosis now have a thoughtful and practical resource to guide and support them through the experience. Hopeful that the voices of those who have to bear the burden of this diagnosis are not just being heard but sought out, valued and provided with a platform. Hopeful that we are creating a better, safer environment for these important conversations.

Kimberley Wilson, Chartered Psychologist, host of the Stronger Minds *podcast and author of* How to Build a Healthy Brain

Preface

I knew I had to write this book when my psychiatrist didn't know of any non-stigmatizing and easy-to-read books to recommend to her patients with borderline personality disorder (BPD). "What books do you think I ought to recommend?" she asked. Whilst I couldn't answer that, I could easily tell her what *not* to recommend. If you are like me and have BPD (or think you may have this condition), then you will understand why a question that ought to be so simple is actually so difficult.

If you're not familiar with BPD, then the first thing you need to know is that it is one of the most stigmatized mental health conditions. One study on so-called 'difficult patients' in mental healthcare found that patients with a diagnosis of BPD were judged more negatively by staff than patients with other diagnoses (such as schizophrenia), even when their behaviour was the same (Koekkoek, van Meijel and Hutschemaekers 2006). The same study states that, when asked about the characteristics of 'difficult patients', psychiatrists mentioned BPD up to four times more often than any other diagnosis. Earlier research describes inpatient mental health nurses being more likely to 'belittle' patients with BPD than those with schizophrenia, and a study from 2007 found that mental health nurses were more helpful to patients with major depressive disorder than those with BPD (Forsyth 2007; Gallop, Lancee and Garfinkel 1989). Too often, people with BPD are perceived as deliberately – and even cunningly – behaving in a 'difficult' manner. As I hope this book will show, this couldn't be further from the truth.

One of the most well known books about BPD is the insensitively titled *I Hate You – Don't Leave Me* by Jerold Kreisman and Hal Straus (1991). Amongst other misunderstandings, this bestselling book claims that a person with BPD 'lacks true empathy' (p.38) and 'use[s] manipulative gestures for display purposes only' (p.236). As if this stereotyping were not hurtful enough, *I Hate You – Don't Leave Me* argues that people with BPD 'represent the fracturing of stable units' in society and 'often rush to singles bars or other crowded haunts, often with disappointing – or even violent – results' (Kreisman and Straus 1991, p.37). Rather than providing any meaningful insight into the feelings and experiences of people with BPD, this book works better as a primer on the stigma associated with the condition. It certainly goes some way to offering a snapshot of why so many people with BPD end up feeling hopeless about themselves and their futures. Although published over 30 years ago, it remains a bestseller in the field.

I Hate You – Don't Leave Me is far from the only book about BPD that reinforces stereotypes and perpetuates stigma. Although these books are well intended, many have titles implying that people with BPD are difficult, destructive or unlovable – *Hard to Love: Understanding Male Borderline Personality*

Disorder (Nowinski 2014), *Stop Walking on Eggshells: Taking Your Life Back When Someone You Care About Has Borderline Personality Disorder* (Randy and Mason 1998) and *Sometimes I Act Crazy* (Kreisman and Straus 2004). As you will know if you have ever looked for a book about BPD, their covers often feature unflattering images such as smashed glass, barbed wire, cracked mirrors and people with two heads screaming. In *5 Types of People Who Can Ruin Your Life*, 'borderlines' are included as people who aren't just hard to deal with; they're seen as dangerous (Eddy 2018). As someone with BPD, is it any wonder that a visit to a bookshop or a library to find information about my condition left me feeling disgusted with myself and demoralized about my future? Although supportive and compassionate books about BPD do (thankfully) exist, they are scarce and usually belong in one of two categories. The first is memoirs so deeply rooted in the circumstances of the author's life that they are not always fully relatable. The second is academic books that are too dense and jargon-filled to grapple with when feeling overwhelmed.

Books that perpetuate stigma are just the tip of the iceberg. Googling 'borderline personality disorder' is often, naturally, the first thing a newly diagnosed person will do. A couple of clicks reveal widespread derogatory attitudes towards the condition online. YouTube videos boasting thousands of views warn that people with BPD are more trouble than they're worth, impossible to connect with and incapable of love. Articles on mental health and psychology websites report the 'drama of loving a borderline' – 'expect a stormy relationship that includes accusations, anger, jealousy, bullying, control' – and that 'borderlines' are 'master manipulators' who 'manipulate their way through life' (Carroll 2019; Lancer 2019). A common theme online is 'how to spot a borderline'. In 2017, *The Guardian* published an article entitled 'Personality disorders at work: How to spot them and what you can do', which was removed following complaints about discrimination.

In 'Fiddler of the truth', Griffiths claims that 'being deceitful' is a 'core' characteristic of BPD and that 'lies are typically told for personal profit or pleasure' (2013). An article offering 'tips' for coworkers of people with BPD states 'you may find a coworker with Borderline Personality Disorder to be manipulative, dishonest, unethical, and willing to cause harm to other employees to achieve their employment goals' (Clearview Women's Center n.d.). These kinds of claims really, really hurt.

Although around one in a hundred people are estimated to have BPD, depictions of this condition in film, TV and novels are less common than portrayals of depression, eating disorders, manic episodes or psychosis (Rethink Mental Illness n.d.). Characters on screen and on page with all manner of mental health difficulties (not just personality disorders) can be problematic and sometimes deeply damaging. Yet, when characters with BPD are actually created, they are often volatile, childish, Manic Pixie Dream Girls, or hyper-sexual, vengeful killers. Even when characters are not explicitly labelled by their creators as having BPD, someone will 'diagnose' them with it. Glenn Close's character in *Fatal Attraction* – who boils a bunny rabbit as revenge – is a notable example (see Meyer-Lindenberg 2009), as is, apparently, Darth Vader, who is also reported to have had BPD (Bui *et al.*

2011). As someone who takes refuge in stories, when I was newly diagnosed I urgently needed a character with BPD who I could relate to and who could give me hope. I never got that character. I am still waiting.

Arguably, the last five years have seen a slight increase in the quantity, and quality, of fictional and real-life representations of BPD. However, progress in representations of BPD (as well as schizophrenia, dissociative identity disorder and other personality disorders) is happening more slowly than in less stigmatized mental health conditions such as depression and anxiety disorders. It is fairly easy to name people in the public eye who have disclosed personal experience of depression, bipolar disorder, an anxiety disorder, an eating disorder or PTSD. However, people in the public eye who disclose BPD are few and far between. Although I have been reading and blogging about BPD for nearly seven years, I can name only a small handful of people in the public eye who have disclosed having this condition.

I understand why so few people, both famous and non-famous, talk about having BPD. Many people, myself included, feel safer disclosing *anything* but BPD. In the past, I would sooner say I had 'traits of bipolar disorder' because I was so frightened of what would happen if I disclosed BPD. Although this made me feel safer in the short term, not being able to speak my truth made me feel (unfairly) like a fraud. The harsh reality is that many spaces and situations are still unsafe – or not fully safe – for people with BPD. In an article for *The Statesman*, a Stony Brook University newspaper, one student explained that the example their psychology professor gave of someone with BPD was a woman who had killed her husband (Frankl 2019). Is it any wonder that people don't feel comfortable telling family, friends, people they're dating, colleagues or even health professionals about their BPD?

Understandably, for many people the risks of being deemed untrustworthy, incapable or even dangerous can be too high. For people who are further discriminated against on the basis of sexuality, race, religion, disability or gender, the price of disclosing a condition as stigmatized as BPD is likely to be even higher. People with BPD inhabit all walks of life, communities, professions and families, yet we often remain invisible. As a person with BPD, I am not only relentlessly misjudged, but also constantly silenced and erased. I am a teacher working with children with special educational needs. Often, the training courses I attend talk about mental illness and trauma as if someone with first-hand experience couldn't possibly be in the room. I am not the other. I am one of you. Speak about me as if I were in the room – because I am.

As if these challenges weren't enough to contend with, people diagnosed with BPD tend to have a harder time accessing professional support (especially effective and relevant support) than those with other diagnoses. In the UK, many areas do not have specialist services for people with a diagnosis of personality disorder. As the Royal College of Psychiatry states, the 'availability of treatment remains more dependent on geography, rather than need' and 'there remains considerable variation in whether services are available, what they offer and to whom' (2020, p.6). In locations that lack specialist services, people with a diagnosis of personality disorder may be supported solely by GPs who 'have little choice to

improvise their own management plans' or possibly be referred into short-term talking therapies that are ill-equipped
to meet their needs, such as IAPT (Improving Access to Psychological Therapies) (French *et al.* 2019, p.1). Furthermore,
it is worth mentioning here that not all IAPT services accept
people with a personality disorder diagnosis. Too often, individuals with BPD can get stuck between a rock and a hard
place, having little to no effective care as described previously,
and then come into contact with emergency services (police
or ambulance) or the accident and emergency department
due to a mental health crisis. Alarmingly, the quality of care
from the police, ambulance service, or accident and emergency departments can vary widely, from compassionate and
thorough to accusatory and traumatic.

In instances when people can afford to pay for support,
there is no guarantee of finding a professional with relevant
experience or who is willing to take a client with BPD. As
one study described, 'people tend to distance themselves
from stigmatized populations, and there is evidence that
some clinicians may emotionally distance themselves from
individuals with BPD' (Aviram, Brodsky and Stanley 2006,
p.249). Specific non-profits and charitable organizations
exist for people with depression, bipolar disorder, psychosis,
OCD (obsessive-compulsive disorder) and eating disorders,
yet dedicated helplines and community support groups for
people with personality disorders are almost non-existent.
Sometimes it feels as though people with personality disorders just don't matter. It breaks my heart that the suicide rate
for people with BPD is high. It ought not to be this way.

I discovered the stigma surrounding BPD the hard way

when, aged 23, I was diagnosed with the condition. Leaden with silence, shame and a lack of specialist support, I started an anonymous blog and Twitter account. It gave me self-expression when I had no one to talk to, and helped me find ways of coping when I didn't know where to start. Initially, I called my blog BPD Orchid, but later I changed its name to Talking About BPD (hence the title of this book!). In the months and years that followed my diagnosis, Talking About BPD gave me a space to make sense of my experiences and connect with others who felt similar. It has been fulfilling to share the reality of my life with BPD, a life that bears no resemblance to the hurtful descriptions and portrayals I have encountered.

In 2017, I was nominated for a Mind Media Award for Talking About BPD. I wanted to attend the ceremony (I love any excuse to dress up!), so knew the time had come to let go of my anonymity. I didn't win the award, but in 2019 I was shortlisted again. To my delight and astonishment, I won. In my acceptance speech, I said that more than anything I wanted people with BPD to be seen for who they truly are and not dismissed as a stereotype. I hope that this book – which in many ways is an extension of my blog – contributes towards achieving this goal. I want everyone with BPD to know that they deserve nothing but compassion, understanding and re-spect, even when faced with the injustices of discrimination, stigma, exclusion and cruelty.

If you have BPD or strongly relate to the traits associ-ated with this condition, then this book is for you. I am not gatekeeping who this book is for, though: if you think it could help you, then it's yours. This book may be especially helpful if your hopes for a calm and happy future are fading embers, or have even completely burnt out. If you have times when you feel worthless, unlovable or helpless (just as I once did), then these pages are here to show that you are worthy of care, you are lovable and that there is hope for your future. Each chapter has been written in the knowledge that you may not have as much professional or personal support as you may like, or need, right now. I am also aware that you may not have an ideal amount of validation or understanding from the people around you. Unlike other books about BPD, this one acknowledges that the agony of BPD is often twofold; first, there is the condition itself; and second, there is the stigma. I could never have written a book about this condition without paying as much attention to stigma as to the particulars of the condition itself.

I know how overwhelming daily life can be for people with BPD. This book contains techniques for managing intense emotions, distressing thoughts, urges to act impulsively, anxiety in relationships and changing feelings about who you are. These techniques are largely based on DBT, but some draw on aspects of cognitive behavioural therapy (CBT) and acceptance and commitment therapy (ACT). I also draw on some creative techniques that I have invented myself over the years. Each chapter shares snippets of personal experience drawn from my life, which I hope will be comforting, validating and help you feel less alone.

Whilst this book may look pretty on a shelf, I wrote it for you to use: cram it in your rucksack to read on the bus, underline key passages with a highlighter and adorn it with coffee stains. Like a reassuring memory, keep it close so that when waves of shame, sadness or fear crash over you, you are reminded that you are not a stereotype. Let this book be a reminder of your worthiness, lovableness and inherent belonging in the world. No matter what you may have read, seen or been told, you are not manipulative, attention-seeking or dramatic. You are not too sensitive, too emotional or too much. You are a person who sometimes feels huge pain and hasn't always known what to do with such agony, a person who deserves nothing less than compassion, understanding and the utmost respect.

CHAPTER 1

What Is BPD?

People with BPD tend to have emotions so intense that they feel painful. Their moods can rise and fall at lightning speed, and they can have relentless anxiety about relationships accompanied by powerful urges to act impulsively. Day-to-day life with BPD can feel frightening, confusing, exhausting and lonely. Some days, every drop of energy is given over to keeping safe from self-harm or staying alive when the idea of suicide seems like the only option. With such an unsettling set of difficulties, it's no wonder that this condition can cause huge amounts of distress for those affected and their loved ones.

Like many people with BPD, I became so used to living in emotional pain that this agony became my normality. After years of feeling suicidal and being on the verge of hurting myself most days, I never dreamed that my life would be as calm and happy as it is today. In the subsequent chapters, I will describe what happened to bring about this change and share techniques you can use to make your life with BPD less distressing and more settled. First, though, I want to address the thorny, and often contentious, question: what is BPD?

Diagnostic and Statistical Manual of Mental Disorders

Arguably, the most influential and high-profile document for categorizing and diagnosing mental health conditions is the *Diagnostic and Statistical Manual of Mental Disorders* (DSM). First published in 1952 by the American Psychiatric Association (APA), the DSM has been through five editions so far (and one revised edition), and is currently referred to as DSM-5. BPD was added to the DSM in 1980 when the third edition of the work was published. As you may know, each disorder listed in the DSM is accompanied by a set of criteria an individual must meet in order to be diagnosed. Before I explain the criteria for being diagnosed with BPD, I think it is important to acknowledge two key debates surrounding this method of categorizing and diagnosing mental health conditions.

Critics of the DSM argue that it unhelpfully, and unfairly, medicalizes responses to difficult experiences or events that are part of being human. For example, someone who has suffered a bereavement as little as two months ago and is showing signs of depression can be diagnosed with major depressive disorder. Many of the DSM's opponents assert that emotional distress is better understood, and treated, by looking at a person's life and the society they live in as a whole, rather than as a mental disorder. Let me explain this with an example. Someone who hears or sees things that others around them don't could, according to the DSM, be showing signs of a mental disorder. However, as the Hearing Voices Movement (HVM) argues, hearing voices is a 'meaningful human experience' (Corstens *et al.* 2014, p.S285). The HVM argues that 'in the majority of cases voice-hearing can be understood and interpreted in the context of an individual's personal experiences', rather than as 'arbitrary content induced by disease' (Corstens *et al.* 2014, pp.S287–S288).

As critics of the DSM highlight, diagnosing a mental health condition involves social, cultural and value judgements. What is 'over-spending'? What constitutes 'inappropriate anger'? Rather than reflecting fixed and universally agreeable truths, these judgements often reflect society and, of course, its power structures. Perhaps the most infamous example of such value judgements is homosexuality, which was originally included in the DSM as a pathology until it was finally removed in 1973 (Drescher, North and Suris 2015). As I will explain later in this chapter, BPD and other personality disorders are strongly contested diagnoses.

The second key debate surrounding the DSM calls into question its relationship with pharmaceutical companies. A 2011 study published in the *British Medical Journal* stated that 56 per cent of the panel members for the most recent edition of the DSM had financial relationships with pharmaceutical companies (Moynihan 2011, p.1054). Additionally, the researcher who chaired the task force for the fourth edition suggested that its panel members not only had financial conflicts, but 'intellectual conflicts' too (Moynihan 2011, p.1054).

Whilst many organizations and individuals take issue with the medicalization of distress and conflicts of interest, others see positives in the DSM. Namely, that its categorization of mental health conditions facilitates relevant treatment and support, as well as remuneration from insurance companies. As I will discuss later, though, many people with a

BPD diagnosis do not have an easy time accessing relevant treatment and support.

How I view the DSM

Overall, whilst I accept the DSM's definition of BPD in the context of myself and my life, my acceptance comes with a few caveats. I have full knowledge that this diagnosis (like many others) is laden with social, cultural and value judgements, some of which are deeply problematic. I am aware that my diagnosis reflects my position in society right now; if I were born into a different era, circumstances or culture, then maybe my experiences would not be labelled as a 'personality disorder'. I see the DSM's definition of BPD as an imperfect description, an inexact framework. I do not grant the DSM the same authority on my mental health as I would give a lab test for diabetes or an X-ray for an infected lung. I appreciate that my emotional experience can never be reduced to a list of criteria.

ILLNESS OR CONDITION?

I choose to call my BPD a mental health condition rather than an illness.

There have been certain periods in my life when I have felt mentally ill for sure. However, most of the time, I don't feel ill with my BPD. As this book shows, my emotions, thoughts, behaviour and relationships can all be affected by my BPD in many different ways, but rarely do I feel ill with it.

The nine criteria for a BPD diagnosis

The DSM-5 lists nine diagnostic criteria for BPD (APA 2013). For an individual to be diagnosed with this condition in the context of this diagnostic framework, they need to meet five or more of these criteria. In 2013, when professionals suggested that I might have BPD, I was confused by what these nine criteria meant, which is why I am going to explain them in everyday language with examples.

Before looking at these nine criteria, though, let me share my summary of BPD based on how the DSM-5 outlines it (APA 2013, p.663). BPD is described as an array of difficulties that are prevalent across a number of areas of a person's life (i.e. family, friendships, romantic relationships, work, leisure). These difficulties are not one-off, isolated struggles, but repeated, ongoing challenges that started by the time a person reached early adulthood. As you will know if you have BPD, this condition involves relationships that are very unsettled, fraught with anxiety or feel very up and down. (It is worth noting that relationships could refer to those with friends, family, peers or colleagues, not just romantic relationships.) To give you examples of the many forms relationship instability could take, think repeatedly breaking up with a partner only to get back together, feeling desperate to be close to a friend and then wanting to get as far away from them as possible or constantly checking whether your boss still likes you.

Another facet of BPD noted in the DSM-5 is having a changing self-image, meaning that you see yourself in vastly different ways over a short space of time. For example, on Monday you might feel good about yourself and believe you have something to offer the world, but on Tuesday you see yourself as worthless, with no positive qualities and nothing to offer at all. Someone with a fluctuating self-image might change their goals or preferences more often than other people, perhaps altering their direction or aspirations in life every few months. If you can relate, you will know how incredibly confusing this feels and how difficult it can be to make decisions about your life.

A further aspect of the condition noted in the DSM-5 is unsettled, up and down emotions and moods. For example, a person with BPD might be laughing one minute and then crying the next. Someone with up and down emotions and moods may feel so depressed in the morning that they cannot get out of bed, but then be jumping around excitedly and feeling joyful in the afternoon. To a person who hasn't lived this reality, I know such intense and sudden shifts in mood might seem impossible. Another dimension to BPD is impulsive behaviour that is so significant that it's noticeable to others around you. I think of impulsive behaviour as doing something in the heat of the moment without stopping to think about the long-term consequences. Impulsive behaviours might possibly involve substances like drugs or alcohol, spending a lot of money in a short space of time or making a big decision (like quitting a job) on the spur of the moment.

Now that I have given an overview of BPD, let's take a look at nine criteria that are commonly used to diagnose this condition. For the specific wording of these criteria please consult the DSM-5 (APA 2013, p.663). It is also worth noting that some clinicians use the International Classification of Diseases (ICD) to diagnose borderline personality disorder instead of the DSM.

- Feeling very frightened of being abandoned. Doing everything you can to stop someone abandoning you, even if there is no actual risk of abandonment; behaving in a fearful or distressed way when trying to stop abandonment happening or when faced with separation. Examples are texting repeatedly to ask 'Do you still like/love me?', feeling extremely anxious when friends go home or feeling distraught when a loved one goes on holiday. This does not include suicidal or self-harm-related behaviours.
- Having a lot of anxiety linked to relationships. Having relationships (with partners, family members, friends, colleagues etc.) that are turbulent, full of anxiety or always unsettled; thinking someone is the 'best person in the world' and then suddenly seeing them as terrible, rather than seeing them as a mixture of both positive and negative qualities.
- Difficulties with your identity. Having a shifting sense of who you are, such as one day feeling very positive about yourself and the world, and the next feeling like you're an awful person and the world is a terrible place; having goals or priorities that often change – one month starting a project with excitement, but the next month wanting to change track; being chameleon-like – changing lifestyle, beliefs, appearance or other characteristics to 'fit in' with social groups; struggling to recall past emotional states, which can make present feelings seem ever-lasting.
- Acting on impulse in ways that could make your life more difficult in the long term. Doing something potentially damaging or that could sabotage your wellbeing

or progress in life without stopping to think about the consequences; acting on urges even though they will not help you in the long term – for example, getting drunk before a nerve-wracking event, even though alcohol will make things harder for you or ruin the occasion. This does not include suicidal or self-harm-related behaviour.

• Doing things associated with ending your life or self-harming. Attempting suicide, making plans to end your life, talking about suicide, writing suicide notes or doing something to show that you are considering suicide; doing something to hurt your body or cause physical pain.

• Emotional instability and fluctuating moods. Mood swings that are very intense and change quickly; experiencing very different emotional states over a period of minutes, hours or days. These mood changes occur in response to things that happen, especially things to do with relationships, for example, feeling despair in the morning when a friend doesn't reply to your text, but suddenly feeling on top of the world in the afternoon when this person calls you. Feeling very irritable, anxious or unhappy for a few hours, but not usually for more than a couple of days.

• Feeling uncomfortably hollow or empty. Having a long-term feeling which, for many people, feels similar to despair, hopelessness or constant dread. Nothing seems to bring comfort or a feeling of safety. Some people liken this feeling to having a pit in their stomach, a void inside themselves or being hollow.

• Finding it difficult to manage anger. Having high levels of anger that are difficult to manage, in particular when feeling rejected, abandoned or ignored by someone, anger that might, on the surface, seem out of proportion to the situation at hand, but that signifies painful experiences or fears, and then acting on these angry feelings by shouting, breaking things, slamming doors and so on. Some (but not all) people with BPD might get into fights when angry.

- Temporary paranoia during times of stress or experiencing dissociation. Feeling suspicious of others, such as thinking that people are talking about you or are plotting to do something unkind to you; finding hidden meanings in body language or facial expressions that others don't see; feeling as though you have left your body and are looking at it from the outside or feeling that you are unreal; feeling detached from your mind, body or the world around you, as though you are behind glass or underwater. These experiences usually only happen during times of intense stress and for brief periods of time.

WHERE DOES THE WORD 'BORDERLINE' COME FROM?

In the decades leading up to the inclusion of BPD in the DSM-III in 1980, some doctors were referring to certain patients as having 'borderline states' or being 'on the borderline' (Stone 2005). Many psychiatrists tended to categorize their patients into two main groups. The first group was people with 'neurosis'. Neurosis largely referred to people thought to have trouble with their 'nerves' and who often felt anxious or depressed.

The second group included people with 'psychosis'. Psychosis described people who were thought to have trouble with their mind (rather than their 'nerves'), and who often thought, heard or saw things that others did not.

Some individuals could not be neatly categorized into either group. This led some psychiatrists to describe these patients as being 'on the borderline' between neurosis and psychosis. The word 'borderline' gained prominence in the 1960s and 1970s when a number of books were published describing a 'borderline syndrome' and 'borderline patients' (Gunderson 2009). BPD is not generally understood in these terms anymore, and there is ongoing discussion about its name and whether other names ought to be adopted, such as emotional intensity disorder or emotional regulation disorder.

Just to add whilst we are on this topic, I know that in psychiatry, 'personality' generally refers to how a person thinks, feels and behaves. I understand therefore how 'personality disorder' came into existence because personality disorders involve a person's thoughts, feelings and behaviours. However, as personality is such an emotionally charged word – often used to refer to the essence of a person's character – the name personality disorder may feel incredibly demeaning.

Everyone with BPD is different

Because a person must experience at least five of these criteria in order to get a diagnosis of BPD, there are 256 possible combinations of symptoms (Mulay *et al.* 2019). Whilst some researchers believe that there are groups of symptoms that tend to cluster together, even a cinema full of people with BPD may have no two individuals with the same combination of symptoms. Plus, even if two people did have the same combination of symptoms, there would probably be differences in their experience of those symptoms. One person who has a fluctuating self-image might swing between feeling good and bad about who they are, but have fixed goals and values. By contrast, another person with the same symptoms might have a solid belief in their inner goodness, but very changeable goals and values.

What's more, even if two people had an identical combination of BPD symptoms and experienced them in a very similar way, they would be different in other respects. One person might be an outgoing, adventure-loving dog owner who runs a bakery, whilst the other might be a quiet scientist who loves learning languages and can't stand dogs. Sometimes people with mental health conditions are incorrectly thought of as all the same. Yet, a person with a mental health condition is an individual with an identity just as complex as someone without mental health problems. My BPD is a big part of me, but there is so much more to me than BPD. Everyone – with or without a mental health condition – has their own set of hopes, fears, beliefs, values and preferences. Don't ever let someone make you think otherwise.

What does my BPD look like?
When I was diagnosed with BPD in 2014, I met all nine criteria. I have always enjoyed having high scores when it comes

to assessments, but this one felt like a different kind of 'full marks'. My main difficulty was fear of abandonment. For many years, I was so distressed by the idea of people I loved leaving me that I would think about suicide and have urges to self-harm. Rarely a day went by during my adolescence and early twenties when I didn't spend at least an hour sobbing in my bed or on the floor. Each episode (as I called them) was excruciating; they would leave me with headaches, puffed-up eyes and marks where my fingernails had pierced my skin. The agony of my episodes was so great that I often thought they would kill me. In fact, the pain during an episode felt so overwhelming that, in that moment, death seemed preferable.

The most confusing aspect of my episodes, though, was how suddenly they came on. Not being able to predict when an episode would arise, I neither trusted my moods nor felt safe in my own body. The speed at which my emotions would plummet and then skyrocket felt impossible to cope with. Even though the walls of my bedroom or bathroom were usually the audience for my episodes, I wondered whether I was inventing them simply for dramatic effect. That's not to say my episodes happened independently of other people. Although I usually managed to suppress my episodes until I was alone, they were generally linked to feeling rejected or abandoned by someone I cared about. This could be the smallest of social interactions: a text without a reply, a pause in a conversation, someone glancing away.

My opinion of myself would shift alongside my mood too. If someone I liked connected with me, I felt valuable. Yet the moment I perceived them disconnect from me, I experienced myself as a shameful and disgusting human being. Criticism was particularly frightening. The second that someone suggested I had done something 'wrong' it felt as though every atom in my body was shattering and I thought I deserved to die. My thoughts of being an embarrassing, shameful or worthless person were often followed by impulsive behaviour as a way of trying to check if I was still valued. Most frequently this was repeatedly texting or calling someone and expressing my panic: 'Do you still love me? Do you still care about me? Do you not like me anymore? Am I a disgrace? Am I disgusting?' I felt as though I couldn't cope.

Even though my emotions and my opinion of myself shifted seismically, my values, interests and goals remained steadfast. I knew what I stood for and what I loved. I relished books, words, anything creative, nature, my family and friends. When I wasn't engulfed by my episodes, I was with my friends, family and peers, laughing, studying, doing something creative and generally enjoying life. The most difficult question I faced was how to reconcile the part of me that laughed and loved so fiercely with the part of me that felt suicidal and had urges to hurt myself. Trying to understand, I drew pictures of myself as a girl with two heads and two hearts, one face smiling, the other crying, one heart beating brightly, the other splintered through its centre.

How would anyone ever believe that I spent hours lying on the floor thinking of dying? I didn't even believe it about myself. I want to make it clear, though, that even though people around me haven't always been able to recognize or understand my difficulties, I have never been uncared for or unloved. In fact, it is the complete opposite. I have always had family and friends who care deeply about me, who love me and who would do anything to help me, and for that I shall be forever grateful.

Another aspect of myself that I didn't understand when I was a child and a young adult was the grim, hollow sensation that sometimes appeared in the centre of my body. I named this feeling 'the vortex' because it felt like a vast black hole capable of swallowing a planet – and that planet was me. After my diagnosis, I realized that this was the feeling of deep emptiness that I had read about. Around the age of 10 my anger ignited too. For a few years, every time I felt wronged, disbelieved or misunderstood, I would scream and shout or run down fields and country lanes. When I was breathless and exhausted, I would cry until something or someone helped me stop. My early teens were a confusing and lonely time. I hated my first secondary school; everything scared me there and I was permanently on edge. I cried in the toilets during break times, had several emotional breakdowns in class and read near constantly so I could imagine I was anywhere else but school. It was the early 2000s and the education system was as competent at supporting students with mental health problems as it would have been at sending a rocket to the International Space Station. When I changed schools, I enjoyed being a student once more, but it didn't remove my mental health problems.

Episodes of paranoia have, thankfully, only occurred during moments of extreme stress. The first time I had paranoid thoughts was as a child when, for a couple of scary moments, I was overcome with the thought that I was going to be attacked. I was prone to nightmares and I knew I had a vivid imagination. Nonetheless, I couldn't understand why my brain could create such horrifying images whilst I was awake. As a teenager, I had paranoid thoughts once in a while too. Now and again, these happened at night-time whilst washing my face. I had vivid images of lifting my head up from the sink and looking into the mirror, where I would see my face smothered in blood like a zombie. When I was at university, during the stress of final exams, I had thoughts that people in the street were carrying weapons that they could use to hurt me.

There were also a couple of occasions when I was texting someone and I became scared that they were going to call the police. Once, I packed an overnight bag and ran out of the house, not knowing where I was going. After about 15 minutes, standing outside a corner shop, I felt more like myself again and took the bus to the crisis team based at the hospital. Undoubtedly, though, my paranoia was at its strongest during two years of living in a house share with friends. Living with people I was so fond of could have been a dream, but from the moment I moved in it became a nightmare. I feared rejection from them constantly; even mundane interactions and decisions made me feel on edge. The constant anxiety about rejection became so stressful that I became paranoid that my friends hated me or were talking about me. I have experienced some dissociation too, but this has only happened during certain types of therapy sessions (as I will discuss in Chapter 6).

I am so happy that today my life is much calmer and happier. My BPD impacts me significantly less than it did a few years ago because my emotions and thoughts are less distressing and all-consuming than they used to be. Yes, I continue to experience intense emotional states, but I know how to bear their force so that they don't overpower me. I am still extremely sensitive to anything that feels like rejection and abandonment, but I feel so much more secure in relationships now. When fear of rejection or abandonment swoops in, I usually know how to pause, assess the situation and consider my response.

Similarly, when my opinion of myself shifts from 'good' to 'bad', I can remind myself that this perception of myself is temporary and that being criticized is part of life. When I am under a lot of pressure or something upsetting happens, thoughts about suicide and self-harm sometimes still arise. Nowadays, though, I know how to make them feel less threatening. Furthermore, I no longer have an intense feeling of emptiness, paranoia is thankfully rare, and so is anger that feels unbearable. I find it moving to think about the vastness of my transformation and how happy I am to be here writing this book today.

These enormous changes were made possible by learning to manage overwhelming thoughts and feelings and making my daily life calmer. Chapter 6 discusses how different therapies helped me achieve this, and Chapter 7 shares some techniques to get you started on creating a calmer and happier life for yourself too.

How do the symptoms of BPD relate to one another?

As you have probably noticed, many of the features of BPD are interlinked. Shifts in mood or self-image, intense anger, paranoia or dissociation can all happen when someone believes they will be abandoned or rejected. Additionally, it makes sense that someone who is continuously scared about abandonment or rejection might have unsettled or difficult relationships.

Fear of abandonment can lead a person to cling to a person they love, and find time alone uncomfortable or even frightening. It may feel easier for some people to push others away, even when problems don't exist, because the idea of being rejected in the future feels too scary. Sometimes people with this fear will prioritize others' needs and wants above their own, as well as stay with people who are not a good match or are even abusive.

One of the most influential psychologists in the field of BPD, Dr Marsha M. Linehan, organized the symptoms of BPD into a number of areas of 'dysregulation' (Linehan 1993). 'Dys-regulation' refers to difficulties with regulating (adjusting or moderating) something. People with BPD often have dysregu-lated emotions, thoughts, behaviours, relationships and feel-ings about themselves. If you have BPD, you may have noticed that one kind of dysregulation can easily lead to another kind. It's as if each aspect of my BPD is a cog in a complex machine; if one cog moves, then it can set the others in motion. For example, if my emotions are dysregulated, then the way I feel about myself is liable to change like the wind. Similarly, if my thoughts are all over the place, my behaviour is more likely to be up and down. When I am worried about my relationships, I tend to think very harshly about myself. For many years, I didn't realize that one form of dysregulation can send the others into a tailspin. Once I realized the interlinked nature of these difficulties, it finally made sense as to why my life felt so painful and why I felt so confused all the time.

COMMON EXPERIENCES OF PEOPLE WITH BPD

In the early days of being diagnosed, I found nothing more comforting than reading something about BPD that resonated with me. I wanted to list some common experiences that people with BPD have that are not always captured by the DSM, medical websites or in leaflets your doctor might give you:

- Feeling like an outsider, or feeling different to everyone else.
- Feeling misunderstood, or like nobody knows the 'real you'.
- Having a 'favourite person' whom you feel you need for safety and happiness.
- Feeling that an emotion will last forever, and believing you will always feel (and have always felt) this way.
- Feeling like everything hurts, and even the tiniest of things can cause huge pain.
- Never feeling safe, and having a constant sense of dread.
- When someone is away from you, it's difficult to imagine that person thinking of you.
- Difficulty relaxing due to being in a state of 'high alert'.
- Frequent reassurance-seeking and checking that things are 'okay'.
- Having vivid or frequent nightmares.
- Holding yourself to standards so high that they are unattainable.
- Exhausted by life with intense emotions.
- Believing that you are unlovable.

A contested diagnosis

As I mentioned earlier in this chapter, BPD is a controversial diagnosis. In fact, BPD and other personality disorders are amongst the most strongly disputed mental health diagnoses alongside schizophrenia, dissociative identity disorder, gender dysphoria and a number of other diagnoses included in the DSM-5. Some people argue that BPD lacks scientific validity and is not a legitimate diagnosis. As the influential researcher in the field of BPD, John Gunderson, describes, BPD has 'neither a specific pharmacotherapy nor a unifying neurobiological organization from which biological psychiatry can find purchase' (Gunderson 2009, p.533). In simple terms, Gunderson is saying that there is no specific medication that has been consistently proven to treat BPD, and no patterns in the brain that can be used to fully define or fully understand the condition.

From the 1980s onwards, individuals raised concerns that BPD reflected men's gender biases towards women, pathologized women and acted as a punishment for those who had been sexually abused. These are issues that continue to be addressed today and call for further discussion. More research is certainly needed on the experiences of women, trans and non-binary people, in particular black and minority ethnic women, who are too often neglected by research studies. Since the 1990s, debate has grown about whether BPD is more accurately understood as a form of post-traumatic stress disorder (PTSD), which continues today. What's more, there is, without a doubt, an urgent need for more research on the impact of racism, poverty, homophobia, transphobia and sexism on people diagnosed with BPD.

Furthermore, some individuals and organizations assert that diagnosing a person with BPD is deeply damaging and unethical. A number of people argue that it blames people who have often experienced trauma for their difficulties and then re-traumatizes them, leading to further emotional distress. Some argue that the diagnosis of BPD is used as justification for maltreatment by, and exclusion from, mental health services. As psychiatrist and psychotherapist Jay Watts writes in the newspaper *The Independent*, the diagnosis of BPD often reinforces 'early messages from outside that one is unlovable, wrong, defective or too much' (Watts 2018). She notes that 'psychiatric staff demonstrably move away from and feel less emotionally connected with people who have been given this label' (Watts 2018). As Watts states in 'Borderline Personality Disorder – A diagnosis of invalidation', it is a diagnosis that is often given to people deemed to be 'too sexual, too clever, too aware of their actions to deserve care, interest and respect' (Watts 2016).

In their 'Position Statement on Borderline Personality Disorder', critical theorist and activist collective Recovery in the Bin (RITB) state that even though they have a neutral stance on diagnosis, they oppose the BPD diagnosis (RITB 2019). This is because they view BPD as 'a special case because of its specific and politicized use' (RITB 2019). RITB attest that the BPD diagnosis is used as a 'reprisal' (i.e. a payback) for people who make a complaint, do not respond to medication or do not recover in ways professionals think they should (RITB 2019). They argue that the BPD diagnosis is given to people in order to accelerate their discharge from mental health services for 'financial and ideological reasons'.

Furthermore, RITB describe BPD as 'a misogynistic diagnosis given to women, transgender and non-binary people mostly due to its links with childhood trauma, childhood sexual abuse or to the sole action of self-harm' (RITB 2019).

My thoughts on the diagnosis of BPD

It is horrific that people with a diagnosis of BPD are commonly excluded from mental health services and mistreated by professionals. It is horrendous that individuals with this diagnosis are often viewed as 'too aware of their actions to deserve care, interest and respect', rather than being offered the support they need and deserve (Watts 2016). Whilst some people believe that the only way to end this discrimination is to take the diagnosis of BPD out of use, at the moment I'm not convinced that this would provide an effective solution to the injustices currently faced by people with BPD.

Would abolishing the diagnosis improve access to relevant care and support for people with these kinds of difficulties? Would it lead to increased respect and understanding for such individuals? I'm not sure it would. Instead, I think it would be more effective to increase the quality and services for people with BPD and make them more accessible. That being said, I admire and respect individuals like Jay Watts and groups like RITB for challenging the usefulness, ethics and validity of BPD as a diagnosis. Their work is certainly amplifying the voices of so many people who have suffered hugely after being diagnosed with this condition.

At times I feel guilty for embracing a diagnosis that some people experience as traumatizing and which has been described as invalid, misogynistic and damaging. However, I have chosen to accept this diagnosis for myself because, as I explain in the next chapter, it has helped me, and has even possibly saved my life. The BPD diagnosis has given me understanding, helped me find relevant treatment and ways of coping, and has enabled me to find others with similar experiences. I do not think that my diagnosis itself is the reason why I have been excluded and discriminated against in the past. I think that the structure of mental health services and the inaccurate perceptions of professionals is the reason for my discrimination and exclusion.

Whilst, ultimately, I think it would be more effective if this criteria-based medical model of diagnosis was replaced with a system that had a more nuanced understanding of emotional distress, this is the only framework that I have available to me right now, and for the foreseeable future. I know that BPD is an unstable diagnosis and I don't know whether it will be still here in the decades to come or whether it will be replaced with something else. I am sure that there could be a better alternative. For now, however, I wear the BPD label in the full knowledge that it is an inexact and rough description of a few aspects of myself, not something that describes every facet of my existence and who I am. Whilst this is my personal relationship with my diagnosis, I urge you to explore your own. I know that many people disagree with how I think of my diagnosis. That difference is okay and fully valid; all I ask for is respect.

CHAPTER 2

How Does BPD Develop?

One of the first questions that people with BPD naturally ask is, 'Why do I have it?' Answering this is tricky because, as is the case with a number of mental health conditions, there is no single identifiable cause. Instead, researchers have identified several possible factors that may interact with one another to cause what is known as BPD.

Two key factors that have been identified as possibly playing a role in the development of BPD are:

- Differences in parts of the brain, especially the areas associated with emotion regulation and impulse control.
- Difficult, traumatic or overwhelming experiences during childhood or adolescence.

This chapter begins by exploring these two key potential factors in the development of BPD. We look at the concepts of 'neuroplasticity', 'invalidating environments', 'insecure attachment' and traumatic experiences, which I hope will bring some clarity, and perhaps even comfort, to you.

Neuroplasticity

As you may know, areas of the brain do not remain the same throughout life, but develop and adjust their activity levels in response to new situations and what's going on in our environment. The ability of areas of the brain to develop and adjust their activity levels is known as 'neuroplasticity'. Let me give an example. A study that looked at the brains of licensed London taxi drivers shows how the brain can adjust to meet demands in the environment (Maguire *et al.* 2000). It demonstrated that London taxi drivers had larger posterior hippocampi, the area of the brain involved in spatial memory, compared to people who were not required to memorize thousands of routes and streets (Maguire *et al.* 2000).

People often ask whether someone is born with BPD, and the concept of neuroplasticity can shed some light on this question. Imagine a maternity ward full of newborn babies. Each of these babies will be born with a brain that is unique in terms of its shape, size and activity levels in different areas. Some of these babies will be more emotionally sensitive, reactive to stimuli or impulsive than others, just as some will be better at problem-solving, learning languages or hand–eye coordination than others. The emotionally sensitive babies on the maternity ward may be more easily over-stimulated by lights, sounds or touch than the less emotionally sensitive babies. They might cry more easily, need more comfort in order to settle, or find certain textures of clothing, bedding or food overwhelming. I was an emotionally sensitive baby for sure.

Let's stick with these babies for a moment. Out of these emotionally sensitive babies, some will grow up in environments that teach them to regulate their strong emotions and sensitivity to stimuli. Although they will still be sensitive individuals to some extent, their brains will develop and adjust in such a way that they will not constantly be overwhelmed. By contrast, some of these babies will grow up in environments that do not help them emotionally regulate or manage their innate sensitivity. As a result, their brains adjust in such a way that their sensitivity, emotionality and impulsivity intensify.

In summary, most researchers agree that people are not born with BPD. Instead, what has come to be known as BPD arises from a complex interplay of factors involving the brain and the environment it develops in.

Invalidating environments

Dr Marsha M. Linehan, the psychologist who created dialectical behaviour therapy (DBT), emphasized the role of the 'invalidating environment' in the development of BPD, an environment in which 'the communication of private experiences is met by erratic, inappropriate, and extreme responses' (Linehan 1993, p.49). In other words, an invalidating environment teaches a child that their thoughts and feelings are wrong, shameful or excessive.

EXAMPLES OF UNHELPFUL AND INVALIDATING RESPONSES

Erratic responses

A four-year-old child is starting school for the first time and is feeling anxious. His parent sometimes responds with empathy and reassurance, but at other times tells him to "Stop whinging, you have nothing to worry about."

The child struggles to know whether his parent will be understanding or dismissive, and so feels safer keeping quiet when he feels anxious.

Inappropriate responses

A 15-year-old girl is having a hard time because she is struggling to make friends at school. Her brother has an illness and is in hospital a lot of the time. The girl's family tell her she is not allowed to cry about "trivial things" when there are "much bigger" problems in her family. As a result, the girl feels ashamed of her emotions and believes she is selfish for feeling this way.

Extreme responses

A 10-year-old child suddenly feels sick in the middle of class. His teacher yells at him: "Why do you always have to disrupt my lesson? You never stop with your drama. Sit down. You can stay behind for 10 minutes." The child learns that expressing his needs leads to punishment.

EXAMPLES OF COMMON INVALIDATING STATEMENTS

- Stop being so sensitive.
- You have no reason to feel this way.
- Other people don't get emotional like this.
- Why do you always have to be so dramatic?
- Get over it.
- Your brother's not complaining, so why are you?
- Stop crying and stop being so ungrateful.

The impact of invaliding environments

Children who grow up in invalidating environments fear being humiliated, punished or dismissed every time they express how they feel. Understandably, they may feel safer trying to understand overwhelming thoughts and feelings on their own, rather than seeking the support of adults around them. Because children don't have the skills or knowledge to regulate their emotions and make sense of the world by themselves, they are likely to come up with incorrect conclusions about what is happening or blame themselves for any difficulties.

In short, invalidating environments do not teach children how to identify, regulate or tolerate emotions effectively. Without the support of validating adults, children also miss out on valuable opportunities for learning how to manage frustration, conflict and disappointment.

Growing up in an invalidating environment can lead to feelings of immense loneliness and shame. When children or young people do not feel safe enough to express themselves, they can feel as though they have a whole secret universe inside themselves that cannot be known about or shared. Trying to contain so much unacknowledged emotion can lead to intense outbursts of anxiety or anger, thus creating further emotional dysregulation and feelings of shame.

Insecure attachment

A number of studies have found links between insecure attachment and the development of BPD. Attachment theory explains how an infant's bond with their caregivers affects their social and emotional development and, in particular, their experience of relationships as an adult. Attachment theory describes several types of attachment.

One type of attachment is known as 'secure attachment', which is characterized by caregivers who respond consistently to a child's signals and accurately understand the child's emotional states. Attachment theory states that children who have a secure attachment with at least one caregiver usually develop a positive, consistent self-image, and view themselves as worthy of love. It also theorizes that children with secure attachments see others as accepting and responsive to their needs.

Another type of attachment is known as 'insecure attachment', which is characterized by parents who respond inconsistently to a child's signals and often do not accurately understand their child's emotional state. Attachment theory describes that children with insecure attachment may feel more anxious and have more difficulty regulating emotions than those who have a secure attachment. Children with insecure attachments may also see others as more unreliable and more difficult to please than children who have secure attachments.

Research by Gunderson (1996) shows that some of the behaviours seen in children with insecure attachments can be seen in people with BPD. These behaviours include checking the closeness of loved ones, seeking reassurance and not wanting to be apart from others, which may be followed by a fear of dependency. As Fonagy explains in his 2010 study, people with BPD are 'exquisitely sensitive to all interpersonal interactions' and usually have 'hypersensitive attachment systems within interpersonal contexts' (Bateman and Fonagy 2010, p.12). As explained in Chapter 6, a number of treatments for BPD focus on building secure attachments and regulating a hypersensitive attachment system so that individuals can develop a more stable, positive opinion of themselves, and feel more confident and worthy of love in relationships.

ARE 'LOVE' AND 'ATTACHMENT' THE SAME THING?

It is vital to recognize that 'love' and 'attachment' are not the same thing. Developing an insecure attachment is not the same thing as being unloved. There are countless reasons why caregivers may not be able to respond consistently to a child's needs or understand the child's emotional states. In many cases, this is completely unintentional or the result of challenging circumstances such as illness or other difficulties.

There are many people with insecure attachments who feel calm in relationships and feel positively about themselves and others. Sometimes, people with insecure attachments may have to spend more time learning how to manage anxiety in relationships and take extra care to be with people who are understanding. As I hope this book proves, this is more than possible.

Difficult or traumatic experiences during childhood and adolescence

Although there is more work to be done in this area, research demonstrates connections between childhood trauma, abuse and the development of BPD. A 2019 study by the University of Manchester reported that more than 70 per cent of people with a diagnosis of BPD reported having at least one traumatic experience during childhood (Porter *et al.* 2020). It found that people with BPD were 13 times more likely to report childhood trauma than people without mental health problems (Porter *et al.* 2020).

Difficult or traumatic experiences during childhood and adolescence are things that happened to make a child or young person feel frightened, in pain, abandoned, unsafe, unsupported or powerless. These difficulties may have been long-term, as well as one-off events, and could have happened where the person lived, at school or in the community. It is impossible to list every kind of difficult or traumatic experience that a person could go through, but some examples include the death of someone close, a parent moving away or having a family member who had a problem that meant they couldn't give the care that was needed.

Abuse of any kind experienced in childhood or adolescence, including sexual, physical or emotional abuse, is likely to be very difficult and traumatic. Neglect, when someone's physical and/or emotional needs are not met, can also be extremely challenging and traumatic. Other potentially difficult or traumatic experiences faced by children and young people include being rejected by their family, school or the community, and being bullied or treated as an outsider. Difficult or traumatic experiences of all kinds can have psychological impacts that carry forward into adulthood. The 'Resources' section at the end of this book is for anyone who is, or thinks they may be, experiencing abuse or neglect.

Is my trauma valid?

Sometimes people think of their own difficult or traumatic experiences as not 'bad' or 'severe' enough to warrant the pain they feel. At times, people judge others' experiences or circumstances as 'worse' or 'more serious' than their own, and then dismiss their distress or criticize themselves for having difficulties. Throughout my late teens and early twenties, I constantly told myself that I had 'no reason' to be in emotional pain. Ultimately, I found there were two main reasons that stopped me from acknowledging and owning painful past experiences.

First, I didn't understand what constitutes a traumatic experience. I believed that traumatic experiences were always observable events that made news headlines, such as plane crashes, armed robberies, war or natural disasters. I couldn't relate to any of these things. Second, I felt as though I needed permission from others to describe my past in a certain way. I didn't feel that I had the right to describe any of my experiences as difficult or traumatic. I felt like a faker.

Definitions of psychological trauma can be hard to pin down and have changed over the years. However, trauma can broadly be described as an event, multiple events or circumstances that threaten a person's psychological or physical safety and leave a lasting impact on their wellbeing (SAMHSA Trauma and Justice Strategic Initiative 2014, p.7). Generally speaking, traumatic experiences produce feelings of intense fear, helplessness and vulnerability. In the last few years, I have learned that it is not the exact details that make an experience traumatic, but how trapped, helpless, powerless and vulnerable it makes the person involved feel. As Carlson and colleagues note, 'the impact of traumatic experiences is complicated because many factors affect individuals' responses' (Carlson *et al.* 2016, p.106), such as early childhood adversity, levels of social support and prior exposure to trauma. I want more people to understand that what gives one person trauma symptoms may leave another person completely unaffected.

Traumatic experiences and their impacts on individuals cannot be measured on a scale, unlike the hardness of a diamond or the intensity of an earthquake. It is therefore vital that you do not criticize yourself or dismiss your pain because what you have been through doesn't feel 'severe enough'. If you felt vulnerable, you felt vulnerable. If you were frightened, you were frightened. If you felt powerless, you felt powerless. I want to say it loud and clear: your feelings and your experiences are valid. Even though I know this, there are still times when I fear being told that I 'have no reason' to be distressed because 'I have had it so good'. However, this is not about what other people think, but about me and my feelings. A while back, I stopped waiting for permission from others to define my own experiences.

Not everyone has conscious memories of traumatic experiences. This could be because trauma happened in very early childhood or made a person feel so unsafe that they do not consciously remember the events or circumstances. Whilst many people with a diagnosis of BPD relate to having had difficult or traumatic experiences during childhood or adolescence, it is important to know that not everyone does. If you don't identify with trauma, the pain you feel today is no less valid. Pain is pain, no matter what.

CHAPTER 3

Being Diagnosed with BPD

For many people, being diagnosed with BPD can be a long, complicated and frustrating process. Before the words 'borderline personality disorder' were ever spoken to me, I had been diagnosed with depression, generalized anxiety disorder and an eating disorder for around four years. I had undergone countless doctors' appointments, completed a year of therapy for my eating disorder and a further few months of counselling. The first time I heard about the condition was during my second year of university. Just two days before I went home for Christmas, my counsellor told me that she thought I might have it.

I had never heard of BPD before, and so I spent my entire Christmas researching the condition online. It was un-festive to say the least. The descriptions of the condition made me feel more frightened, confused and alone than ever before. I didn't understand and had nobody to guide me. I was suicidal – in and out of the A&E department as directed by transient doctors and people on the end of helplines. Seven long months passed until I finally saw a psychiatrist who could assess me for this diagnosis.

I think I might have BPD – what should I do?

Often, the first step towards being diagnosed with BPD is to speak with a doctor. Many people who are concerned that they might have BPD will have already spoken to a doctor about mental health problems. They may have been previously diagnosed with another mental health condition. Some conditions, such as depression and anxiety disorders, can be diagnosed by doctors who do not specialize in mental health. However, some conditions, like bipolar disorder, schizoaffective disorder, dissociative identity disorder and personality disorders like BPD, require diagnosis by doctors who specialize in mental health, such as psychiatrists.

If your doctor thinks that you may have BPD, they may refer you for an assessment with a mental health team. Unfortunately, many doctors lack training in personality disorders, which can mean some people's possible symptoms go unnoticed. Furthermore, some doctors may be reluctant to help their patient pursue a BPD diagnosis if they believe it is an invalid diagnosis that could harm their patient (see Chapter 1).

An assessment for BPD may happen within days or weeks, although many people may be placed on a waiting list that is months or even years long. When I was in my early twenties, there were times when doctors referred me for immediate mental health assessments, but I had to wait many months for an assessment for BPD. At one point, I was even removed from the waiting list without being told.

It's also important to recognize that not everyone is diagnosed with BPD via their doctor. Some people may be diagnosed whilst they are an inpatient in a mental health unit or through a mental health professional they see privately. It is also worth knowing that, in the UK, children and young people under 18 are not generally diagnosed with BPD. However, if a professional thinks an under-18 might have the condition, they may be described as having 'emerging' BPD. The NICE (National Institute for Health and Care Excellence) guidelines for BPD state that when a person with a learning disability is thought to possibly have BPD, then their assessment and diagnosis must also take place in consultation with learning disability services (NICE 2009).

What happens during an assessment for BPD?

A psychiatrist or clinical psychologist will usually carry out assessments for BPD. They will be completed either in a single session, usually lasting an hour to an hour-and-a-half, or over a series of sessions. Ideally a diagnosis will be carried out over a few sessions so that the professional has more time to get to know the individual.

During an assessment, the professional will ask questions about the kind of distress you experience, how it feels and what you do. Often, they will discuss your relationships, how you see yourself, and whether you have noticed any patterns as to when and how your mood changes. As well as exploring how you feel in the present, the professional will probably ask you how you have felt in the past and your childhood experiences. They will also determine whether you need further assessments for other conditions, or if they are unsure whether you have a condition that can appear similar to BPD (such as bipolar disorder, PTSD or attention-deficit hyperactivity disorder, ADHD).

Without a doubt, assessments can be anxiety-provoking, exhausting and overwhelming. I have always found it helpful to do something relaxing afterwards when I am feeling frayed around the edges. Before having an assessment, it can be helpful to write down a list of things to mention or any questions, in case you (quite understandably) become flustered during the appointment. Some people find it helpful to track their emotions and moods on a chart over a few weeks or months and bring it along to the appointment.

COPING WITH WAITING LISTS

When I was 19 and in the midst of depression and an eating disorder, the waiting list for therapy was over a year. When each day brought a fresh dose of distress that I didn't know how to handle, this was devastating news. My heart goes out to anyone in distress who is on a long waiting list.

More recently, I handled a six-month wait for DBT by reminding myself that each day of waiting brought me closer to something that might help me. If you are on a long waiting list, I recommend contacting the service now and again to check you are still on the list, and to get an update on the estimated waiting time.

Is it BPD or another condition?

Some symptoms of BPD can be similar to those of other conditions including, but not limited to, bipolar disorder, complex post-traumatic stress disorder (C-PTSD) and ADHD. At times, people may be diagnosed with BPD when another diagnosis more accurately describes their difficulties, and vice versa. Professionals should take the time during assessments to ensure that each diagnosis accurately reflects the difficulties of the person in front of them.

In some instances, BPD and bipolar disorder are mistaken for one another. One study found that almost 40 per cent of patients diagnosed with BPD reported having a previous misdiagnosis of bipolar disorder (Ruggero *et al.* 2010). As Fruzzetti explains, this confusion is 'most likely due to some similarities between symptoms: impulsive behaviour, intense emotions and suicidal thinking' (Fruzzetti 2017). As these two conditions usually have distinctly different treatment methods, accurate diagnosis is incredibly important.

Furthermore, some people find that their experiences are more accurately described with a diagnosis of C-PTSD than BPD (which also tends to be a less stigmatizing diagnosis). C-PTSD can develop in people who experienced repeated trauma, especially if the trauma happened at an early age, was inflicted by someone close, 'lasted for a long time' and 'escape or rescue were unlikely or impossible' (Mind 2021). Symptoms of C-PTSD can be similar to those of BPD, including feelings of shame or guilt, difficulty regulating emotions, suicidal thoughts and relationship difficulties. Additionally, others find that other diagnoses such as ADHD or autism spectrum disorder (ASD) are more accurate descriptors.

People with BPD often have other mental health conditions or difficulties as well as their BPD. When a person has two or more conditions they are known as 'comorbidities'. Conditions that are often 'comorbid' with BPD include depression, eating disorders, PTSD, anxiety disorders (such as panic disorder or OCD), addictions and bipolar disorder (Biskin and Paris 2013).

Common feelings after being diagnosed with BPD

For many people, being diagnosed with BPD can induce a confusing concoction of emotions. Being diagnosed with any mental health condition can be unsettling, but being diagnosed with one of the most stigmatized, misunderstood conditions can feel beyond difficult. This was certainly the case for me.

When I was diagnosed, I worried that my future would cave in and I would have to abandon all hopes. I feared that my plans of a career with children might be ruined, that I was too difficult to love and that my meltdowns would break any connections I had with people. Simultaneously, though, relief flooded through me. It was liberating that my suffering had finally been acknowledged as something other than low self-esteem, exam stress and burn out. My fear and relief were also laced with anger. Why had it taken so long for my pain to be recognized? Why had I been left on my own to navigate a system that didn't see me? Additionally, sadness was ballooning inside me to the size of a blue whale. Now that I had an explanation for my distress, I didn't know where to turn or how to process it. I was lonely and confused.

Of course, following diagnosis every person with BPD

will have their own set of emotions. These emotions will depend on factors such as the support a person has, beliefs about the diagnosis, how the diagnosis is delivered and the events leading up to diagnosis. However, you might recognize some of your own feelings in the descriptions that follow.

Anger

Anger is a common and natural emotion following a diagnosis of BPD. This could be due to disagreeing with the concept of personality disorder and believing that the diagnosis unfairly places blame on the individual and is an invalid diagnosis (see Chapter 1). There could also be anger about the name 'personality disorder' – that in layperson's terms seems to describe your personality as 'disordered' or 'wrong'. Some people feel angry about the sheer amount of time it can take to get a diagnosis. It is frustrating to think of how much time I spent on waiting lists, advocating for myself during consultations and even just trying to book appointments.

It is also understandable to have anger about a lack of support you may have had in recent years or in the past. Sometimes, being diagnosed with BPD raises questions about the lasting impact of difficult or traumatic experiences in childhood and adolescence. Understandably, individuals may feel angry at not receiving the protection and care they needed earlier in life. This is all even before mentioning how angry stigma and discrimination can make a person feel.

Shame

As I discuss in detail in Chapter 7, shame arises when a person believes that there is something wrong with who they are and fears rejection. In my experience, this emotion is often tangled up with fear of abandonment. When I was first diagnosed with BPD, I largely hid my diagnosis because I believed nobody would want to love me, hang out with me, work with me or support me if they knew about my BPD. Saying the words 'borderline personality disorder' aloud made me feel so disgusted that I wanted to vomit.

I trace my shame back to the moment I was diagnosed. The psychiatrist who assessed me told me that she wasn't going to record my diagnosis in my medical notes. That way, she explained, I could be free from negative judgements by medical professionals. Whilst she was trying to protect me, her decision had the opposite effect. It made me feel like BPD was my 'dirty little secret'. I hid it from professionals for several years because I was scared of what they might do if they knew about it. It stopped me from seeking help when I needed it most. I know that it was well meaning but, honestly, I wish that my diagnosis had been delivered to me in a different way. In the days and weeks following diagnosis, shame can hit hard due to increased exposure to negative media representation, stereotyping by the public or mental health professionals, or exclusion from services.

Relief
Some people feel relief after being diagnosed with BPD. It can be validating to learn that your difficulties can be understood as part of a mental health condition and they are not the result of a personal failing or character flaw. As an adolescent, I wondered whether I was imagining my mood changes or inventing my suicidal thoughts just because I was 'difficult'.

It was affirming to see that my distress was real – and always had been.

Having a name for your pain can bring comfort. Finding a word for my experiences meant I could use that word to find others online with experiences that reflected my own. Ultimately, this showed me that I wasn't alone. For the first time since adolescence, I stopped feeling abnormal.

Sadness

Being diagnosed with BPD can bring about intense sadness for many people. A few months after I was diagnosed, I noticed that I had suffered through a decade of self-harm, suicidal thoughts and rollercoaster moods without any accurate treatment or understanding of what was happening. This realization made me feel incredibly sad. Whilst my past is full of happy memories, it is also marked by unattended mental health problems – a city strewn with colourful garlands whose walls are punctured with bullet holes.

As I will explain in Chapter 7, sadness is characterized by feelings of loss, disappointment and helplessness. All of these are natural following a diagnosis of BPD. It is understandable to grieve lost opportunities, the help that didn't come or the time spent in despair.

Fear

People who are newly diagnosed with BPD can, understandably, feel fear and anxiety about their new diagnosis. It can be terrifying to feel judged and misunderstood as a result of stigma or discrimination, especially when it comes from people in positions of power such as doctors or social workers.

Many people are scared that the negative judgements about BPD are true, and fear for what their future holds. I hope that by the time you reach the end of this book you will know that the stereotypes about BPD couldn't be further from the truth.

Sometimes people feel anxious because they don't know what to do with this new knowledge: I have a diagnosis of BPD, now what? This is especially likely for people without consistent or helpful professionals who can guide treatment and care.

Hopelessness

It is understandable for anyone with a diagnosis of BPD to feel, at times, devoid of all hope. As I have already mentioned, people with BPD face the double challenge of stigma on top of the condition itself. I felt hopeless when I was first diagnosed with BPD because I thought I might have to let go of my dreams, and I feared I would never know how to cope. This turned out not to be the case. A few years later, I have everything I could have wished for and more: a loving relationship with my partner, a fulfilling career, solid family relationships and friendships, as well the satisfaction that Talking About BPD brings. In spite of what some people might say, there is so much hope for people with BPD to feel calmer and have fulfilling lives.

As I go on to describe in Chapter 6, there are a number of treatments for BPD that can reduce distress and make life calmer. I know that these are not always accessible to everyone at any given moment, but, as explained in Chapter 7, there are coping techniques that can help you to manage painful emotions and feel more settled when professional support is missing. Please know what I didn't when I was newly diagnosed: there is hope, things can feel better and you do not have to drop your dreams.

Struggling to access support after being diagnosed with BPD

As I mentioned in the Preface, the availability and quality of mental health services specifically for people with BPD vary widely. Whilst some mental health services are equipped with teams that specialize in personality disorders, others, frustratingly, have no dedicated provision. Whilst BPD has been described as 'no longer a diagnosis of exclusion', unfortunately, in some locations, it still very much is (NIMH 2003). When I was first diagnosed, I wasn't offered any support specific to my BPD after diagnosis or even a follow-up appointment to ask questions. Although I had regular counselling sessions and doctors' appointments, neither my counsellor nor my doctor was able to offer me any advice or treatments tailored to my BPD. I felt as though the psychiatrist had handed me a map I couldn't decipher – and there was no one to ask who could even tell me which way up to hold it.

Over the years, I have consistently encountered mental health professionals who seem to know little about BPD. In 2013, when a doctor had arranged for me to see the crisis team because I was suicidal, I mentioned to two mental health nurses that I thought DBT could help me. Even though DBT is perhaps the most established therapy for the treatment of BPD, the nurses had never heard of it. In this moment of vulnerability, I felt embarrassed to know more about mental health treatments than the people who were supposed to be looking after me. I was despairing that anyone would, or could, ever help me. Even when suicidal, the system wasn't equipped to help me.

If you are not offered support following diagnosis, try to ask your doctor or other healthcare professional why this is. Unfortunately, many people with BPD are burdened with having to advocate for care when they are at their most vulnerable and exhausted. I wish I had more advice for people who are struggling to access support. However, I do have the following tips:

TIPS TO ACCESS SUPPORT

- Although repeated rejection can make it feel impossible, please keep asking for help. Change doctor if you can. Get a second opinion. Go back and ask again later in case the structure of services has changed. If you move house, ask for help again in your new area, because it may be more accessible.

- Use the 'Resources' section at the end of this book for advice on navigating the system or finding other sources of support.

- Get creative. Pursue all possible avenues of support with an open mind. Try helplines, charities, community organizations and online support groups. If one doesn't work for you, don't give up – try the next one. Over the years, my approach has had to be 'throw enough mud at the walls and sooner or later some of it will stick'.

- Remember, not being given support is not a sign that you are undeserving of help. It is a sign of an

---

inadequate mental healthcare system and society that does not (yet) do enough to help people with mental health problems.

CAN I CHALLENGE MY DIAGNOSIS?

There are numerous instances of professionals diagnosing BPD without making individuals aware of their new diagnosis. As illustrated by the Mental Welfare Commission for Scotland report into the experiences of people with BPD, one in ten people consulted described finding out their diagnosis by accident, for example by 'being copied into an e-mail by mistake' or when requesting copies of medical documents (Mental Welfare Commission for Scotland 2018, p.16). This can be very upsetting and in my opinion, completely unethical. At times, some professionals make a diagnosis too quickly without taking the time to fully understand a person's experiences. I think this is completely unacceptable too.

There are a number of reasons why a person may want to reject a BPD diagnosis. I mentioned some of these reasons in Chapter 1 when I explained that BPD is a contested diagnosis. If I felt that my difficulties could be more accurately described with a different diagnosis, or I knew that another diagnosis would enable me to access relevant support, then I would consider challenging my diagnosis. To do this, it can be helpful to seek the support of a trusted health or social care professional (if possible), or even some informal support from a friend or family member if you have someone who may be able to assist.

CHAPTER 4

The Stigma Surrounding BPD

Sometimes I think the hardest part of having BPD is not the intense emotions or the fear of abandonment, but how ashamed the stigma has made me feel. In the iconic book *Stigma: Notes on the Management of Spoiled Identity*, Erving Goffman writes that stigma is an 'attribute that is deeply discrediting' (1963, p.3). In other words, stigma is a thing that damages a person's reputation or disgraces them. More recent research describes stigma as a form of power that can be used to keep people with mental health problems 'down, in or away' (Link and Phelan 2014, p.1). Put simply, stigma forces people with mental health problems to hide, stay silent or keep away. I can't help but think of how opportunities for connection, enjoyment and fulfilment have been missed as a result.

Stigmatized people can be discriminated against in person-to-person interactions via prejudices (negative attitudes not based on facts) and stereotyping. They can also be discriminated against by the structures and institutions in society that make policies and hold the power, such as law, healthcare, education or the police. Examples include not being offered a job because of a mental health condition, being denied healthcare or being treated inhumanely by law enforcement. According to the Mental Health Foundation (2015), of all people with long-term health conditions or disabilities, people with a mental health condition face the most problems finding work, decent housing and being socially included. If you have experienced stigma and discrimination, you are not alone. Let me now share some of my personal experiences and how they affected me.

My encounters with stigma
"It's like Dr Jekyll and Mr Hyde"
In my last few months of university, after a long stint in the library preparing for my final exams, I went to grab a much-needed coffee with a friend. Only a couple of weeks earlier I had been diagnosed with BPD and I decided I would tell her about it. 'Why should I have to stay silent about something that means so much to me?' I thought.

Deciding to tell some of my friends about my diagnosis hadn't been an easy decision to make. After weighing up the pros and cons of keeping it secret, I concluded that I felt more comfortable sharing my diagnosis than holding it back. Furthermore, weren't the anti-stigma campaigns telling me that it was 'good to talk', and that mental health problems didn't have to be hidden?

"So, you know I've been seeing doctors and having counselling for mental health problems," I said as casually as I could. My skin felt sticky all over. I hoped I wouldn't vomit across the table. "Well, a few weeks ago I had an assessment.

Turns out I don't have depression and anxiety; I have this other condition called 'borderline personality disorder'."

I had said it. Those three scary words: Borderline. Personality. Disorder.

"Oh yeah, I know BPD," she replied, "It's like Dr Jekyll and Mr Hyde."

Let me pause here. If you don't know *The Strange Case of Dr Jekyll and Mr Hyde* (Stevenson 1886/2002), allow me to explain. It's a book about a scientist, Dr Jekyll, who turns himself into a man called Mr Hyde. As Dr Jekyll, he is respectable and decent, but as Mr Hyde, he is violent and murderous. The kinds of violent acts this person commits as Mr Hyde include trampling on a little girl, beating people and murder.

As quickly as I could, I made an excuse to leave and rushed back to my student room. When my head finally lifted off my soggy pillow, I thought I would never again feel safe enough to tell people about my diagnosis. Dr Jekyll and Mr Hyde...is that how people would see me now? Ever the bookworm, I decided to do my own research. I went to a legal deposit library (a library holding a copy of every book published in the UK) and I summoned the small number of books with 'borderline personality disorder' in their title that had been published in the UK since 2000. Every page I turned unearthed further layers of stigma. Chapter after chapter told me that people with this diagnosis create havoc in romantic relationships, stir up conflict at work and are reckless parents. I read that they self-harm as manipulation and talk about suicide as a 'threat'.

I hoped the internet would offer a different picture of BPD. It didn't. There was an infinite scroll of YouTube videos

with titles like '[...]The Impossible Connection: Loving Someone w/ Borderline Personality Disorder [...]' (Rosenberg 2014),
'Borderlines Will Cause Devastation to Your Sanity and Self-
Esteem' (Surviving BPD Relationship Break Up 2020) and
'Shutting Down Your Borderline Ex: Chainsaw Style' (Elam
2016). One video even had a picture of a zombie to depict
someone with BPD. On the one hand, I knew these descriptions were inaccurate, unfair and often misogynistic. I had
only ever had honest intentions and tried to care for others,
hadn't I? On the other hand, I felt terrified. Was I sucking the
life out of my family and friends? Was I a terrible, horrible
person? At times, this internal conflict felt almost unbearable.

"Leave, or we will call the police"

The stigma I encountered wasn't only confined to books and
the internet; it translated seamlessly into my interactions
with mental health services. Some of the cruellest treatment
I have ever been subjected to was in A&E when I was a young
adult. A doctor had sent me to the crisis team there because
I was suicidal and didn't know how to keep myself safe. If
10 is the most distressed a person can be and 1 is the least
distressed, I was a solid 9½.

Two mental health nurses escorted me along corridors
of people with open wounds, broken bones and suspected
blood poisoning. The destination was a cramped, windowless
room where I was questioned. The nurses interrogated me
as though I had been found with bloodied hands at a crime
scene. Why was I suicidal? Why couldn't I be happy? Why
didn't a "clever girl" like me know how to cope?

They acted as though in 10 minutes they knew everything

about me and my life. I was suffering from low self-esteem, apparently. They would add me to a seven-week waiting list for a self-esteem workshop. Shaking and sweating with fear, I explained that a self-esteem workshop in seven weeks' time wasn't the help I needed right now. I told them that my doctor had sent me to A&E because I was suicidal *right now* and needed help *now*. The nurses told me that I was "refusing the help being offered" and so needed to leave. I expressed again that I was suicidal, felt really frightened and didn't know how to manage. They had no reply except that I was not cooperating and needed to leave.

Anyone who has been suicidal, asked for help and been turned away will know this agony. It flung me to the floor, where I landed with a smack and writhed in terror. I was howling at the nurses' feet, begging for help. Any morsel of compassion they had thrown at my feet, I would have licked off the floor like a stray dog and dragged myself home. Instead, they told me that my yelling was "frightening the patients" and if I didn't leave immediately, they would call the police to remove me.

I got off the floor and walked out into the darkness.

Frightening the patients – But what about me? Wasn't I a patient too? What about how vulnerable I felt? My safety? My feelings? They did not matter. I did not matter.

It has taken nearly a decade to recover from this trauma. Three years passed and I had moved to another city before I dared ask a professional for help again.

"The nicely dressed lady"

I have been misunderstood by people who were supposed to

understand more times than I can remember. One psychiatrist used a hand gesture indicating wrist cutting when she asked whether I self-harm, and called out "Don't do anything silly" as I left her consulting room. On another occasion, a mental health nurse told me that I "shouldn't" feel suicidal because I have a loving family, friends, a job and "beauty". "You have it all, so don't waste your time feeling like this." Wow. If only emotional distress were so simple! If only the love of my family, partner and friends, my fulfilling career, my degree certificate and my shiny hair made me immune to emotional distress!

My self-awareness, intelligence and how 'put together' I am have been used as excuses for why I don't need help. At the same time, I have been deemed as too difficult, risky or challenging to support. Sometimes I have felt that as a person with BPD I cannot win. Why have I spent hours planning my clothes and make-up for an appointment with a new psychiatrist? Will blusher and a bright dress make me look too 'put together' to be offered help? Sometimes I have felt like wearing something a bit dirty, just so the report doesn't state 'The young lady presented with a neat appearance and arrived well dressed in a floral skirt.' I know appearance can be an indicator of distress for some people, but I look the same no matter how I feel. My colourful necklace is just my colourful necklace. I would prefer it if professionals stopped using my clothes and make-up to make clinical judgements. Oh, and whilst I'm on the topic, telling me I'm "too nice to have BPD" is not a compliment.

Stigma and privilege

I am a disabled woman living with arguably one of the most stigmatized mental health conditions. I also have multiple privileges and forms of power as a result of being white, middle class, straight, cis-gender and able-bodied. These multiple privileges and forms of power have given me protection, status and agency as a person with BPD and in my life as a whole. In other words, it is very likely that I experience far lower levels of stigma and discrimination than people with BPD who don't benefit from the privileges and power that undeniably benefit me.

Let me illustrate this point. In their briefing paper 'The Impact of Racism on Mental Health', the Synergi Collaborative Centre states that 'ethnic minority people, when compared to White British people, are more likely to report adverse, harsh or distressing mental health experiences and poorer outcomes when in contact with mental health services' (Bhui *et al.* 2018). In 'On the Realities of Being a Black Woman with Borderline Personality Disorder', Christine Pungong describes being 'gaslighted, patronised, ignored, or just completely forgotten about' by the mental health system (2017, p.116). She asks why all people with BPD are treated as 'undeserving of care', and explains that 'being a black woman adds an intense extra dimension to that' (2017, p.117).

Stonewall's *LGBT in Britain – Health* report highlights the inequalities that LGBTQ+ people face in health services, including mental health services. Participants in the report describe having been told by professionals that their sexuality or their gender expression are to blame for their mental health problems (Bachmann and Gooch 2018). According to research from the Scottish Transgender Alliance, 63 per cent of trans people had experienced a negative interaction such as being belittled or ridiculed for being trans within mental health services (McNeil *et al.* 2012).

When researching this book, I found very few studies on how BPD stigma varies depending on protected characteristics such as race, gender, religion, sexuality, disability or socioeconomic status. This speaks volumes in itself. Whilst much more needs to be done to counter the stigma that hurts people with BPD, it is vital that these efforts do not disproportionately benefit the privileged groups that wield the most power in society. Attempts to reduce mental health stigma must urgently – without fail – address the intersections of race, gender, class, sexuality, disability and socioeconomic status.

Examining the stereotypes

I wanted to share my view on some of the most common stereotypes about people with BPD.

Stereotype #1: People with BPD are attention seekers

As discussed in Chapter 1, people with BPD tend to feel emotions very intensely – sadness can be experienced as crushing despair, and happiness can be an overwhelming feeling of joy. When a person with BPD is panicking or crying, it's not because they are being dramatic; it's because they are genuinely distressed and doing what they can to cope with those feelings.

Referring to someone in emotional distress as an attention seeker fails to see a person in pain and acknowledge their attempt to cope. Behind the thoughts, emotions and behaviour of someone in distress is often a strong need for safety, connection and comfort. Everyone deserves to be listened to, respected and taken seriously.

Stereotype #2: People with BPD are manipulative

Unfortunately, people with BPD often have their behaviour mislabelled as 'manipulative'. As manipulation is the deliberate attempt to control someone's behaviour using dishonest tactics, this judgement is rarely accurate about people with BPD. In my experience, when people with BPD want something from someone (time, support, to meet up), they ask upfront. People who are being manipulative usually conceal their attempts to control others and pretend to have honourable intentions.

Let's look back at my story of being in A&E from earlier in this chapter. It would be easy for my behaviour to be labelled as manipulative: "She can threaten suicide and scream like a baby all she likes, but I won't give her what she wants." Yet, there was nothing manipulative about my behaviour because I was neither trying to use underhand tactics nor conceal my true intentions. Even if I had wanted to craft a cunning plan, I wouldn't have had the thinking power when I was so distressed. I was suicidal and I asked for help. Asking for something is not being manipulative.

"BUT I AM MANIPULATIVE…"

Whenever I tweet that people with BPD are not manipulative, several people with the diagnosis reply that they are. Although everyone is free to describe their behaviour in their own words, I wonder if calling yourself manipulative is a result of being stereotyped and believing it to be true. Of course, there are people with this condition who use manipulation, but this is not a characteristic of BPD. Any distress-related behaviour described as manipulative needs to be renamed as a matter of urgency, especially when this judgement is cast by a mental health professional. If you have been described as manipulative when you were in pain, please know that you are not.

Stereotype #3: People with BPD will never feel better

When BPD was added to the DSM-III in 1980, there was little evidence on how the lives of people with this diagnosis tended to progress. However, a number of long-term studies carried out over 20 years or more found that most people with BPD 'improve with time' and that 'their prognosis is often better than expected' (Biskin 2015, p.305/p.303). Research suggests that difficulties around self-harm and suicidality tend to improve the most quickly, whereas interpersonal symptoms such as fear of abandonment and rejection may take longer to resolve (Zanarini *et al.* 2007).

When I was first diagnosed, I thought that I would be acting impulsively on painful emotions forever. I never dreamed that my life would be as calm and happy as it is today. It would have given me some relief when I was going through the hardest times with my BPD to know that it wouldn't be that painful forever. I hope that reading this reminds you that things can get better.

Stereotype #4: People with BPD are 'difficult patients'

In 2016, I phoned an organization that matches individuals to private therapists. I summarized my difficulties to the staff member, she told me the fee, and said she would find out which therapists were available near me. Just before the call ended, she asked me if I had a diagnosis, so I told her that I had been diagnosed with borderline personality disorder. The tone of the conversation changed. As I had BPD, I would have to see one of their senior therapists whose rate was double that of the standard-rate therapists. I know that BPD is a very serious mental health condition and that there is a shortage of professionals who work with people with personality disorders. However, at the moment of disclosing my diagnosis, therapy suddenly went from affordable to unaffordable. The scope of my difficulties had not changed, only the name I had given. I had been branded a 'difficult patient' not because of my actual difficulties, but because of my diagnosis. I felt crushed.

There are a number of reasons why some mental health professionals may be unable to work with people with personality disorders, such as a lack of dedicated training in how to support people with personality disorders, not having the skills or enough supervision. Research points out 'patients diagnosed with borderline personality disorder can raise anxiety in health professionals' (Warrender 2015, p.623). I can't help but wonder how much of this anxiety relates to the 'challenge' that people with BPD pose and how much relates to the perceptions of this patient group. I noted in the Preface that a 2006 study on so-called 'difficult patients' in mental healthcare found patients with a diagnosis of BPD 'were judged more negatively by staff than patients with other diagnoses, even when their behaviour was the same'. Similarly, when asked about the characteristics of 'difficult patients', psychiatrists mentioned 'borderline personality disorder' up to four times more often than any other diagnosis (Koekkoek *et al.* 2006). Similarly, Woollaston and Hixenbaugh state that patients with BPD are perceived by nurses as 'a powerful, dangerous, unrelenting force that leaves a trail of destruction in its wake' (2008, p.703).

If you work in health or social care, then you will probably have heard someone being described as 'refusing to engage'. It angers me when I hear people being described using these words because it usually signifies a service that is not meeting someone's needs rather than a person who is deliberately being unresponsive. Instead of judging people with BPD as 'difficult patients', services need to ask themselves whether it is they, in fact, who are the ones making things difficult, and if they are offering people with BPD the support they need and deserve.

Stereotype #5: People with BPD are too 'damaged' to help others

There is still a myth that people with mental health conditions are too 'damaged' to be in helping roles such as doctors, nurses, carers, psychologists or teachers. People who have experienced, or still experience, emotional pain can – and frequently do – help others. A notable example is Dr Marsha M. Linehan, who developed DBT, the first evidence-based treatment for people with BPD. In a *New York Times* article, Dr Linehan shared that she spent over two years in a psychiatric facility as a young woman. She explains that she developed the therapy she needed for many years, but never had: 'I was in hell. And I made a vow: when I get out, I'm going to come back and get others out of here' (quoted in Carey 2011).

In the past, I struggled to reconcile my desire to help others with having a BPD diagnosis. As I mentioned in the Preface, I'm a special education teacher who has worked in both mainstream and special schools. Throughout my career, I have received nothing but praise from staff and families in relation to my work. I am a warm-hearted, empathetic person who is a caring friend, partner and family member. Yet I have worried (and still worry sometimes) that people will judge me as incapable or unreliable, even when there is no evidence to suggest this. I guess that this is stigma at its worst, and one of the reasons why I am writing this book. I hope more people can see that it is possible both to have BPD and to be a caring and responsible individual.

Stereotype #6: People with BPD are incapable of having happy relationships

It breaks my heart when people with BPD want happy, fulfilling relationships but believe that this is impossible due to their diagnosis. As you may know, there is a prejudice that people with BPD are too fragile, dramatic, needy, volatile and, in short, too much like hard work to have happy relationships. This stigma extends into relationships of all types, including family, friends and work, as well as medical or therapeutic relationships. Before I started DBT, I could easily overwhelm friends with my overflowing emotions. Even though I never intended to make my friends feel powerless, worried, exhausted or frustrated, I didn't know how to stop this from happening, which left me feeling ashamed and even more unlovable. Since learning techniques to regulate my emotions, I don't overwhelm people like I used to sometimes. It is such a relief to feel more able to cope. Yet, looking back at the times loved ones felt overwhelmed by me, I wish I had been able to see through the shame I felt. I wish I had known that I was still kind, lovable, loving and all those things I wanted to be.

From personal experience and speaking with others, it seems that the strongest stigma about BPD and relationships concerns romantic relationships. For many years, I thought that I would only be able to have a happy romantic relationship if I no longer met the criteria for BPD. I believed that nobody could love me because I cried too much, panicked too much, hurt too much, felt too much and even loved too much. Whilst some people feel that they are 'not enough' for others, I always felt that I was 'too much'.

In the months after I met my partner, I was surprised to learn that he had fallen in love with me for the person I am today. In the context of our relationship, crying was a sign of empathy, not fragility. To him, panicking simply meant I was feeling anxious, not that I was being 'needy'. He doesn't see my expressive and affectionate nature as 'over the top', but as evidence of thoughtfulness and generosity. This relationship has completely reframed how I see myself. There is no such thing as being 'too emotional'. I believe it's a question of finding people who respect, understand and celebrate the qualities that make you who you are.

Stereotype #7: BPD only affects women

BPD can affect anyone, regardless of gender. Whilst 'three times as many women as men are diagnosed with borderline personality disorder' (Harvard Health Publishing 2019), some studies suggest that women are possibly more likely than men to be diagnosed with BPD as a result of clinicians' gender biases (Sansone and Sansone 2011). In other words, professionals may be associating BPD disproportionately with women, rather than more women actually having the condition. Researchers have also argued that the statistics may be misleading due to 'sampling bias', as women are more likely than men to be found in psychiatric services where the studies usually take place (Sansone and Sansone 2011).

Reframing the stereotypes

It has been seven years since I was diagnosed with BPD. In the last few years, I have reframed the stereotypes. I use this list wherever stigma bites to remind myself that I am someone with intense emotions, and not a stereotype.

- ✗ People with BPD are attention seekers and will do anything to get attention.
- ✓ People with BPD often experience intense distress. It's only natural that a person's behaviour will reflect how distressed they feel inside.
- ✗ People with BPD are manipulative. They use dishonest tactics to try to control others.
- ✓ People with BPD are not inherently manipulative. Manipulation involves dishonesty. Therefore, if someone has honest intentions, they are not being manipulative.
- ✗ A person with BPD will always have BPD. They will never feel better.
- ✓ People with BPD can, and do, feel better over time. Accessing treatment can be a struggle, but whilst you are pursuing or waiting for support, there are things

you can do to help manage your emotions and make life calmer.

✘ People with BPD are difficult patients.

✓ The phrase 'difficult patient' says more about a service than the patient. It reflects a service's inability to meet a patient's needs rather than anything about the patient. It is a very unprofessional judgement.

✘ People with BPD are dangerous.

✓ There is no evidence at all to suggest that people with BPD are dangerous. The vast majority of people with BPD are caring people who try hard to avoid hurting others.

✘ People with BPD cannot work in helping professions or care for others because they are too damaged.

✓ The first effective therapy for people with BPD was designed by Dr Linehan, who had experienced the symptoms of BPD herself. There are many people with BPD who are skilled at looking after others as part of work or family life.

✘ People with BPD are incapable of having happy relationships.

✓ It is perfectly possible to have BPD and have happy relationships. Many people with this condition enjoy fulfilling relationships and can be great friends, partners, family members and parents.

CHAPTER 5

Talking about BPD

Not everyone wants to talk about their BPD or is safe to do so. Whilst talking about BPD can lead to empathy, support, connection and a feeling of liberation from hiding, it can also have risks. I feel that some anti-stigma campaigns can increase the pressure on individuals with mental health problems to be open. I would never judge someone who chooses not to be open about their BPD, especially because some people are in stronger positions than others to manage any negative repercussions of talking.

Should I talk about my BPD or not?

If you are not sure whether to be more open about BPD, it might be useful to consider the possible positives or negatives of talking about it. This list is a starting point for thinking about the possible pros and cons for you and your circumstances.

Possible positive outcomes of talking:

- Empathy from others.

- Receiving emotional or practical support from others.
- Feeling liberated from concealing BPD.
- Finding others with similar experiences.
- Feeling more connected to others.
- Understanding yourself better as a result of conversations with others.
- Building stronger relationships due to others understanding you better.
- Being able to receive 'reasonable adjustments' for your BPD under the Equality Act 2010.
- The opportunity to help others understand BPD and change perceptions of the condition.

Possible negative consequences of talking:

- Discrimination such as the loss of your job or housing (which is illegal under the Equality Act 2010).
- Being harassed or abused because of your diagnosis (also illegal under the Equality Act 2010).
- Being rejected by peers, friends, family or colleagues.
- Being stereotyped and unfairly judged.
- Being criticized for being open and told to shut up.
- Feeling out of control and wanting to 'unsay' it but not being able to.
- Feeling worse or having a crisis as a result of any of the above.

Everyone will feel differently about each of the pros and cons above depending on their life experiences and circumstances. Some people will be in a stronger position to manage negative consequences (should they happen) than others. When

I stopped being anonymous on my blog in 2017, I felt able to deal with any negative repercussions. However, two years previously, I was asked by a film crew to participate in a short film about BPD. I declined the offer because, at that time, I didn't feel comfortable talking without anonymity.

There is no right or wrong when it comes to being open. Openness is also contextual, and what feels comfortable in one situation may not feel comfortable in another. I don't talk about my BPD at work, but I am happy to talk about it on my blog. There are some friends with whom I talk about it a lot, and others less so. The only thing that I believe *is* wrong when it comes to openness is judging others for how much or how little they talk about their mental health. That's their business and nobody else's.

How do I know if it's safe to talk?

When I started talking to more people in detail about my BPD, I found certain 'clues' helpful for working out whether someone was 'safe' to talk to. Before being able to recognize these clues, however, I needed to know what a safe conversation looked like. For me, I knew this meant being fairly certain that I would not be called an attention seeker, a drama queen or be shamed for talking. In order to work out what a safe conversation looks like to you, first, identify any fears you have about talking. These could be fears about hearing things that remind you of past trauma or worries about being misunderstood or pitied. From there you can work backwards to find out what 'safe' looks like. For example, if you are worried about being pitied, then you know to speak to someone who will not feel 'sorry' for you.

I can never be fully certain about how someone will

react to me talking about my BPD. However, there are some clues I use to make an educated guess as to whether someone will be understanding and supportive:

- Talking about others respectfully, especially those who are different from themselves or who are often stigmatized.
- Previous instances of talking about mental health problems respectfully.
- Previous instances of talking about physical health problems, disability or neurodiversity respectfully.
- An ability to listen to others with different points of view to their own.
- A readiness to talk about unfamiliar topics that they might not understand.
- Seeing themselves as equal in value to others, rather than as superior.
- A willingness to acknowledge their own vulnerabilities and difficulties.

Writing this chapter brings back a memory from the summer of 2017. I was sitting in the garden of a local pub with two friends trying to find the courage to tell them about my BPD for the first time. When one friend went to the bar, I told the other friend as casually as I could that earlier on I had been for an appointment because I have BPD. I recall the shame and anxiety of saying those three letters out loud to him. When the friend returned, I told her that I was just saying that I had been to an appointment for BPD as it's a mental health condition I have. They were both non-judgemental and laidback about the fact I had told them. It was quite a short conversation that I was glad of, as we had plenty of other chat to cover. Plus, I needed to go to the toilet to cry tears of relief for a few minutes.

MY TIPS FOR HAVING CONVERSATIONS

- Ask yourself if there is a particular time of day when you find it easier to talk. It's better for me to have conversations in the morning because my emotions tend to be more intense in the evenings when I'm tired.
- Write down the key ideas you want to communicate if you feel you might forget your words. I keep all sorts of notes on my phone.
- Choose a place where you won't be interrupted or overheard if those are concerns for you. I have met friends in cafés where it's so silent that the person behind the counter can hear every word of the conversation. If I'm talking about something personal in public, then I need some level of background noise so I don't feel self-conscious.
- Know that you can stop the conversation at any point. You could say, 'It takes a lot of energy for me to talk about this, so I need to have a rest now' or 'It would be good to pause this conversation for now, but maybe we can continue another day if you can.' If the person pressures you to carry on talking, you have every right to walk away.
- Always remember that sometimes people may not want to, or be able to, talk about your BPD with you.

- Talk in a location that you can leave easily if you need a break. If you have a conversation in the first 10 minutes of a long car journey and you then need some time alone to process the discussion, you may be stuck feeling uncomfortable for hours.

- Use whatever medium works best for you, whether that's in person, by phone, instant messaging or letter. In most instances, the mode of communication that is least likely to lead to misunderstandings is face-to-face conversation due to the presence of body language, tone and facial expression (although see below).

- Feel free to practise talking about your BPD anonymously or on your own first. You could call a listening line such as the Samaritans, record yourself talking into the voice recorder on your phone, write a journal or simply talk to yourself when you're alone. You could also do what I did and blog anonymously about your experiences – but make sure to follow internet safety protocols when online.

FACE-TO-FACE OR VIA TEXT?

I have felt judged for having difficult conversations by text, but sometimes it was the only way I was able to express something. I know that face-to-face conversation has elements that texting lacks, but sometimes texting is the only medium that feels bearable. Given the things I have been through, face-to-face can just feel too intense or frightening. There have been times when the choice was silence or texting – and texting has stopped me from hurting myself many times. Some of my most meaningful conversations have been via text, and I honestly don't think this form of communication should be scorned. I really wish nobody had to feel embarrassed for expressing difficult things via text, rather than doing it face-to-face.

Talking to friends and family

Just as some performers feel less nervous with an audience of people they don't know, some people find it easier to talk about difficult things with strangers than with family and friends. There is usually more at stake when talking to someone close than talking to someone unknown. First of all, judgements or negative comments hurt more when they come from someone whose opinion we value. Second, talking about emotive topics with people who care can become very emotional for everyone involved. The techniques explained in Chapter 7 can be really helpful for regulating emotions that arise as a result of difficult conversations.

Talking to friends and family about difficulties can be especially hard for people with BPD due to fear of abandonment and rejection. I have often felt frightened about revealing things in case the disclosure has a negative impact on the relationship. It has taken a long time for me to accept, but I now know that if someone rejects or abandons me because of what I have to tell them, then they are not a person I need in my life.

In spite of my fears, I knew that I needed to choose

speaking over secrecy. Years of silence had made me feel like an imposter, as if my friends and family didn't know the real me. I felt as though all the love I had in my life was only for the parts of me that people knew about, not all of me. When I became more open, this love did not disappear. I learned that all of me was lovable, even the aspects that I thought made me unlovable.

Talking at the start of a romantic relationship

Talking to someone you're dating or starting a relationship with about BPD can be particularly daunting. Before I told my now partner about my BPD, I identified three reasons why I felt so anxious:

- My fear of being rejected by someone I like on a romantic level is stronger than someone I like in a non-romantic way (as it often is for people who don't have BPD too).
- I was scared of being rejected without even having a chance to show myself.
- I wanted to tell this person sooner rather than later. However, as I hadn't known him for very long, it was harder to predict his reaction.

Before I met my now partner, I had vowed to myself that if anyone I dated said anything negative about me or my BPD, then I would walk away immediately. I couldn't risk repeated stereotyping or anyone chipping away at my confidence. When I told him, though, he was so understanding and open-minded; he is my strongest ally and support.

MY TIPS FOR DISCLOSING BPD AT THE BEGINNING OF A RELATIONSHIP

- Only talk when you feel ready, but don't wait until you are 10 miles deep into the relationship. Waiting longer could make it harder to walk away from the person if they react negatively to your disclosure.
- Explain that BPD affects everyone differently, and give a bit of information about how it affects you.
- Describe what helps you manage. If they are supportive, they will be keen to know what they can do to make things easier for you.
- Emphasize that BPD is one of the most stigmatized mental conditions surrounded by hurtful myths and stereotypes. Explain that it is important to get information about BPD from compassionate, respectful sources.
- If they respond negatively and unkindly, walk away. Someone who is unsupportive at the start of a relationship will not change as the relationship progresses. Allow yourself time to feel sad or angry. Remind yourself that there are people out there who will be supportive.
- If you cry or feel overwhelmed when someone reacts in a caring manner, that's okay. At first, I cried all the time when my partner validated my emotions. I felt happy for my present self, whilst remembering all that my past self had lacked.

Talking to children

Sometimes parents want to protect their children from their own mental health problems by not explaining things or pretending their difficulties don't exist. However, when children do not have explanations from a supportive adult, they are liable to come up with their own explanations. Dismissing a child's questions ("It's nothing, darling, I'm not crying" or "Don't be so nosy, go outside and play") may lead to them blaming themselves ("Mummy is sad because of me") or thinking something scary is happening ("Mummy is crying because Grandad is in hospital again").

More supportive responses will praise a child for showing care ("It's so kind of you to ask why I'm crying") and acknowledge their concern ("I can see you are concerned about me, thank you"). Giving an explanation that is tailored to their level of understanding helps reassure a child that they have done nothing wrong and that they are safe: "I'm crying because I'm sad that Auntie isn't coming to the party. Do you remember I told you that I feel very emotional sometimes, and that's why I visit the doctor? Shall we play together for a few minutes?"

There is a hurtful myth that people with BPD cannot be supportive parents. However, there is no reason why someone with BPD can't be a supportive parent if they have strategies in place to manage their mental health so they can meet their child's needs. Most schools have teachers who specialize in child mental health who can give advice about explaining mental health problems in a child-friendly manner.

Talking to people at work

If possible, try researching the laws in your country or state regarding disclosure of mental health difficulties to employers and any protections or support you may be entitled to at work. In the UK, my condition is defined as a disability under the Equality Act 2010, which means I am entitled to 'reasonable adjustments' at work if I need them. I don't currently have any adjustments, but in the past, for example, I asked to leave work half an hour early so I could make it to my DBT group session in time.

I am lucky to have had a very fulfilling career. I have always been in a people-focused role of some kind – teaching assistant, mainstream class teacher, volunteer helpline counsellor, support services coordinator and special educational needs teacher – as well as completing a Master's in Medical Humanities. Throughout my career, I have had a small number of panic attacks at work that have left me feeling very embarrassed. Supportive workplaces will understand that people have varying mental health needs and will make space for calming down. I have always found it helpful to keep workplace conversations about my mental health straightforward and matter-of-fact, especially because my BPD does not impact my ability to do my job (in fact, I think it makes me better at my role!).

MY TIPS FOR TALKING ABOUT BPD WITH AN EMPLOYER
- Before you talk to your employer, work out why you are disclosing. Is it because it is essential information for safety reasons, or because it impacts your ability to carry out your role? Is it in order to request 'reasonable adjustments' for a disability? Is it so an

employer knows why you had time off or why your approach to work has changed? Is it simply because you feel more comfortable telling them? All of these are completely valid reasons for speaking to your employer.

- Acknowledge how anxiety-provoking it can be to disclose a mental health condition in the workplace. It is normal to feel anxious talking about BPD given its stigma, and being nervous is not a personal weakness.

- Consider talking to a colleague you get on with about your condition before formally telling a manager. When I was feeling very nervous about talking to a manager, I was reassured to know that I had an ally in the building who already knew about my BPD.

- Write down what you want to say if it will help you express yourself in the moment.

- Identify where you can learn more about your legal rights in case your disclosure results in unfair treatment. Although employers are becoming fairer and more educated about mental health problems, unfortunately discrimination still happens.

- Allow yourself time to unwind at the end of the working day. Make a plan to do something calming.

Coping with negative reactions

I've had many conversations about my mental health that felt humiliating, painful and chaotic. However, I've had many more that have been comforting, restorative and possibly even life-saving. I wanted to end this chapter with some thoughts that may provide comfort in the event of negative responses to talking about BPD.

- If someone deems you an 'oversharer' or criticizes you for 'talking too much', please know that you don't need to shame yourself. There is nothing wrong with wanting to talk about your life or your experiences, especially if you haven't had an opportunity to do this before. In my opinion, the use of the word 'oversharing' can be blaming and controlling.
- Individuals who lacked validation in the past often crave large amounts of validation. Of course, it is helpful to find a balance, but please don't be embarrassed if finding a balance is hard sometimes.
- Judgemental comments say more about the person speaking them than they say about you.
- I have had many conversations in which my emotions have become overwhelming. I have been left feeling extremely embarrassed about crying, panicking and impulsive behaviours. In these cases, reassurance didn't take away my shame; my main healer has been time.
- People who have been shamed by others for being open may shame themselves when they are honest. Notice that this shame has taken root inside you, but it comes from elsewhere outside of you.
- It takes courage to talk about BPD in a society that still stigmatizes mental health conditions. If you can, celebrate yourself for being vulnerable and honest because it takes huge strength.

CHAPTER 6

Treatments to Help with BPD

The main kind of treatment for BPD is psychotherapy, which I will refer to as 'therapy' for short in this chapter. Therapy usually involves talking with a therapist about thoughts, feelings and experiences in order to help a person deal with problems, feel less distressed, and live a more contented and fulfilling life. Therapy can be carried out on a one-to-one basis or as a group, family or a couple. Treatment may be time-limited (for a set number of sessions) or open-ended (no exact time limit given when sessions start). Some types of therapy are highly structured according to a manual (guidelines for how the therapy needs to be carried out), and others have a more free-form structure. Some kinds of therapy focus on what's happening in the present, whilst others examine past experiences and their impact on how a person feels today. Some types may explore a person's past and present experiences in combination.

Psychotherapy can be life-changing for people with BPD. There are many therapies that people use to manage their

BPD, and, unfortunately, I haven't got the space to list all of them in this book. According to Choi-Kain *et al.* (2017), there are five types of therapy with an 'evidence base' for treating BPD (if a treatment has an 'evidence base', this means that it has a body of research demonstrating its effectiveness). The therapies covered in this chapter that have an evidence base for treating BPD are dialectical behaviour therapy, mentalization-based treatment, transference-focused psychotherapy, schema-focused therapy and Systems Training for Emotional Predictability and Problem Solving. Let's take a look now at these five evidence-based therapies used to treat BPD.

Evidence-based therapies for treating BPD
Dialectical behaviour therapy
One of the most well known therapies for BPD is dialectical behaviour therapy (DBT). DBT was developed by Dr Marsha M. Linehan from the 1970s onwards to help people experiencing self-harm, suicide attempts and suicidal ideation. It has been extensively used since the early 1990s to treat people diagnosed with BPD.

DBT is adapted from cognitive behavioural therapy (CBT), which focuses on behaviour change. However, DBT differs significantly from CBT because it places equal importance on acceptance, as well as on behaviour change (in fact, the word 'dialectic' in the therapy's name means a balance of opposites!). In DBT, the therapist validates an individual's thoughts, feelings and behaviours at the same time as teaching them how to change. The therapist aims to blend acceptance ("I understand why you hurt yourself") with change ("Let's work on your distress tolerance skills").

DBT is a manualized therapy that centres on learning 'DBT skills' across four modules: mindfulness, emotional regulation, distress tolerance and interpersonal effectiveness. Although DBT acknowledges the impact of invalidation or trauma on emotional regulation, for the most part it examines an individual's present situation rather than delving into the past. DBT is generally carried out as a time-limited therapy of between six months and two years in duration.

Treatment usually involves a weekly group session led by two therapists and a weekly one-to-one session with a therapist. Group sessions involve training on how to do DBT skills, as well as group discussion about this learning, and one-to-one sessions that explore an individual's difficulties and their use of skills. DBT also includes 'phone coaching' (phone or text support) by the one-to-one therapist throughout the week if needed. Phone coaching provides in-the-moment opportunities for a person to learn how to apply DBT skills to difficulties as they arise in between sessions. I will share my life-changing experience with DBT later in this chapter.

Mentalization-based treatment

Mentalization-based treatment (MBT) is an established therapy for treating BPD based on learning to 'mentalize' effectively and consistently. 'Mentalizing' is the ability to recognize and understand that our behaviours and those of others are influenced by mental states. Imagine I'm walking down the street and I see a friend. I say "Hi" to her, but she doesn't respond. If I conclude that she is deliberately ignoring me because she doesn't like me, then I am not mentalizing well. Reflecting on the several possibilities for why she didn't respond (headphones in, distracted, tired, too noisy) would be more effective mentalizing. As you can imagine from this example, a strong capacity to mentalize aids understanding and communication between individuals, supports emotional regulation and strengthens an individual's sense of self. By contrast, not mentalizing effectively can increase misunderstanding between individuals and lead to further emotional dysregulation.

The theory of mentalizing is rooted in attachment theory, which states that a child's bond with caregivers affects their social and emotional development (see Chapter 1). Anthony Bateman and Peter Fonagy, the creators of MBT, explain that BPD is strongly associated with interrupted attachment. They state that 'the most important cause of disruption in mentalizing is psychological trauma early or late in childhood', which affects the 'capacity to think about mental states' (Bateman and Fonagy 2010, p.12). As you may have noticed, though, individuals with BPD can often be noticeably strong at mentalizing when their emotions are not heightened and they are not under stress. In fact, as a special education teacher, I have a strong capacity to understand that a child's behaviour is driven by their mental state. Mentalizing can be seen as the basis for empathizing, which is something that many people with BPD can do very well.

However, there are specific circumstances in which I am liable to lose my capacity to mentalize effectively. This usually happens when I am under stress, during communication with people very close to me and when my emotions are heightened. For example, if a friend doesn't reply to a message, I sometimes jump to the conclusion that they don't like me rather than exploring other possible (and more plausible) reasons why they haven't responded. MBT teaches people to mentalize consistently, especially in emotionally challenging situations, in order to reduce emotional dysregulation, impulsive behaviour, self-harm and suicidality.

MBT is an integrative form of psychotherapy, which means that it draws aspects from several kinds of therapies (including psychodynamic, cognitive and systemic therapy). Like DBT, it is a manualized, time-limited therapy that usually lasts one to two years involving a weekly group session and a weekly one-to-one session.

Transference-focused psychotherapy

Transference-focused psychotherapy (TFP) is a form of psychoanalytic psychotherapy that explores deeply buried thoughts and feelings, especially those from childhood. TFP was designed by Otto Kernberg and colleagues in the 1970s and 1980s specifically for people with BPD. As its name suggests, TFP pays close attention to the 'transference' between the client and therapist. In therapy, transference refers to how the client feels and thinks about the therapist based on their previous experience of relationships, especially early relationships. For example, someone who was criticized throughout childhood by family members and teachers might experience their therapist as a punishing figure, even when the therapist is being neutral or supportive.

TFP uses the transference to help an individual to better understand themselves and others in order to create lasting personal change. There is evidence to show that TFP can reduce suicidality, self-harm, and help people develop a stronger relationship with themselves and others. It is a highly structured, manualized therapy usually involving one-to-one sessions twice weekly for at least one year.

Schema-focused therapy

Schema-focused therapy (SFT), also known as schema therapy, was created by Jeffrey Young in the 1990s. Young noticed that individuals with longer-term difficulties such as personality disorders often responded less well to CBT than those with shorter-term or more fluctuating difficulties. As a result, Young decided to create schema therapy by integrating aspects of CBT with more in-depth psychotherapeutic approaches designed to address difficulties that developed during childhood.

Schema therapy uses the term 'early maladaptive schema' to describe patterns of feeling, thinking and relating that are self-defeating. According to schema therapy, early maladaptive schemas develop as a result of 'unmet needs' during childhood. For example, a child with unavailable caregivers may have unmet needs in terms of emotional connection, leading them to develop an 'abandonment/instability' schema. Schema therapy recognizes 18 schemas, including 'defectiveness/shame', 'punitiveness' and 'self-sacrifice'.

Schema therapy involves an exploration of a person's early maladaptive schemas followed by 'limited re-parenting' facilitated by a warm, secure attachment between the therapist and client. Schema therapy aims to help a person create healthier schemas that will make life less distressing and more fulfilling. This kind of therapy normally involves one-to-one sessions, but it can also be carried out as a group.

It is normally carried out in an open-ended manner that may take three or more years for people with BPD.

Systems Training for Emotional Predictability and Problem Solving

Systems Training for Emotional Predictability and Problem Solving (STEPPS) is group-based treatment designed for people needing support with emotional regulation such as individuals with BPD. STEPPS was designed by Nancee Blum in the 1990s as a supplement to individual psychotherapy, rather than as a standalone treatment. STEPPS is largely a psychoeducational treatment, meaning that participants learn about emotional regulation and techniques to manage their emotions, thoughts and behaviours in order to lessen distress.

STEPPS combines elements from CBT with 'skills training', which can be likened to DBT skills learning. STEPPS also has a 'systems component', which means that there is an opportunity for an individual's family members or loved ones to also learn about emotional regulation. It is a manualized and time-limited treatment involving weekly group sessions over 20 weeks, making it much shorter than other time-limited therapies such as DBT. STEPPS can be delivered by professionals such as nurses or social workers, even if they are not trained in psychotherapy.

Other psychotherapies used for people with BPD
Cognitive analytic therapy

Cognitive analytic therapy (CAT) examines patterns of thinking, feeling and behaving that developed in an individual's past, and asks whether they are helpful in the present. It focuses particularly on difficulties in relating to others. CAT has a growing evidence base for its efficacy for people with BPD.

Cognitive behavioural therapy

As one of the most widely available therapies for a range of mental health conditions, cognitive behavioural therapy (CBT) is sometimes offered to people with BPD. Whilst certain elements of CBT can be useful for some individuals with BPD, some professionals argue that it does not fully address the type and depth of difficulties that many people with BPD face.

Acceptance and commitment therapy

This therapy teaches mindfulness and acceptance strategies along with techniques for living a life consistent with personal values. Acceptance and commitment therapy (ACT) emphasizes the value of staying in the present moment (as opposed to ruminating on the past or worrying about the future) and psychological flexibility (being able to think about possibilities, rather than thinking rigidly). At present, there is only a small body of research on ACT for people with BPD.

Art psychotherapy (art therapy)

In art psychotherapy (or art therapy), individuals are encouraged to express themselves and communicate through drawing, painting, using clay, collage or other visual media. Art therapy is not about creating an artistic masterpiece. Instead, the creative process and images are used as tools for insight, dialogue and personal growth. Whilst many people with BPD have art therapy sessions, there has been little research into its effectiveness for people with BPD.

Therapeutic communities for BPD

Some people with BPD spend time living in a 'therapeutic community'. Therapeutic communities are places where people with long-term conditions live, or spend a significant amount of time, together with the support of healthcare staff. They are highly structured places with clear routines and rules that focus on mutual support and developing positive social relationships. Therapeutic communities usually have a specific focus, such as personality disorders, other mental health conditions, addictions, people who have been in the criminal justice system or learning disabilities.

Therapeutic communities often involve group therapy, individual therapy and creative therapies, as well as chores and shared recreation such as exercise, cooking or gardening. Some people may live in a therapeutic community full-time for a year or two, whereas others may spend time there a few days a week for a year or two. Members of a therapeutic community can learn from one another, as well as professionals, with the aim of building fulfilling lives and increasing their emotional wellbeing.

My experience of therapies

Over the last 10 years, I have done quite a few different types of therapy, from generic counselling to CBT, psychodynamic therapy, ACT and DBT. The first type of therapy I did was CBT when I was about 20, which focused on my eating disorder. The CBT was successful in as much as it pretty much ended my eating disorder, but what it didn't do was resolve any of my underlying distress or emotional dysregulation.

In 2010, severe mental health difficulties meant I had

to pause the degree I had just begun and spend 10 months almost entirely in bed. When I went back to university to resume my much-loved studies of poems and novels, I received some wonderful support from both academics and the pastoral team alike. However, as my difficulties didn't fall under the umbrella of exam stress, difficulty adjusting to life away from home or even depression and anxiety disorders, I sometimes felt university-based services were not equipped to deal with me. One counsellor peered over her clipboard and suggested that perhaps my degree just wasn't the thing for me. I felt hurt and misunderstood; I loved my subject fiercely, and knew that my mental health problems had nothing to do with it. Similarly, I attended a handful of support groups, but talking about hurting myself, sobbing in the street and swinging from feeling suicidal to laughing wasn't relatable to other group members. Even amongst people with mental health problems, I felt like I didn't belong.

In 2013, I decided to start weekly therapy by a counsellor who offered student rates. It felt good to have someone non-judgemental to talk to, but – again – this wasn't the right type of support or nearly enough to meet my needs. I struggled through 2014 and 2015 without professional help after the harrowing experiences I described in Chapter 4, but the following year I decided I would find a private therapist to help me cope. The therapy agency I spoke to told me that I would have to pay a higher fee because I had a personality disorder diagnosis. I couldn't afford the higher rate and I felt desperate, so I called back another day without mentioning my diagnosis and was offered an appointment at the standard rate.

As I sat in this therapist's beige consulting room scattered with seashells and pinecones, I thought that if I told her about my BPD diagnosis, she would turn me away. To be turned away again (to be seen as 'a difficult case') after everything I had been through honestly felt like it might kill me. This type of therapy was psychodynamic, which meant looking at past experiences, and I wasn't at all prepared for its special kind of agony. Each session pared another layer from me until I felt like a prawn, peeled and sizzling in hot oil.

Excavating memories was so painful that I dissociated most sessions. As I briefly explained in Chapter 1, dissociation can be a response to things that feel traumatic, unsafe or emotionally overwhelming. I felt detached from my body as though I were floating above the chair and had a bird's eye view of the seashells and pinecones. On a few occasions, I thought the lamp was flickering, and when I asked my therapist if it needed a new lightbulb, she didn't know what I meant. Many sessions left me in such distress that my therapist had to ask me if I could get home safely. Most of the time, I didn't know whether I could or not. A few times, I walked down streets feeling so lost and lonely that I thought my heart was broken. Although this therapy gave me some insight, it made me feel even less safe in my own mind and body, and it gave me no relief from my BPD at all.

It was DBT that finally offered me the support and solace I needed. 2016 had brought a flurry of crises that left me unable to cope. Following an army of appointments with a battalion of staff, I started my 18-month wait for this therapy. It was 10 years too late, but I can safely say that it changed my life. Almost immediately after starting DBT, there was an improvement in my emotional regulation, as well as my ability to cope with suicidal thoughts and urges to self-harm. After years of being told "Stop sending texts", "Stop crying on the floor" and "Stop hurting yourself", DBT taught me how to manage. My emotional dysregulation was seen and understood, rather than judged; my everyday terror was acknowledged and validated, instead of misunderstood.

DBT lifted my bruised and battered heart out of my chest, held it and soothed it. I no longer saw myself as a chaos-causing monster, but as someone who had been through so much and was simply trying to survive. I learned that my BPD was not my fault and nobody was to blame; it had arisen from a 'perfect storm' of factors. The trust I had in my DBT therapist was far stronger than any previous professionals I had seen. I could let my guard down with her because her therapy was rooted in the real world. She wasn't afraid to recognize the stigma associated with personality disorders or to acknowledge the role that injustice – sexism, racism, homophobia, transphobia and more – can play in emotional distress. How refreshing it felt to find a therapy so brave, unapologetic and relevant, compared to the others I had done that felt so neutral, detached and intangible.

In DBT, I never dissociated whilst discussing painful topics or went home feeling suicidal because my therapist made sure I knew how to keep myself safe in the present moment. Although my therapy sessions were infused with gentleness and humour, they were bold in their requirements. They demanded courage, commitment and grit. My therapist would look me in the eye and tell me that I needed to face my fears, both of us knowing full well that I had the skills to succeed. Those two years of DBT changed my life.

Medication

Although there are no medications licensed to treat BPD, many people with a diagnosis of BPD are prescribed certain medications by medical professionals in order to help with certain mental health difficulties they are experiencing. Over the years, I have taken a few medications for my mental health difficulties at various times with mixed results.

I have tried several types of antidepressants at different stages, mostly to help with suicidal or anxious thoughts. There are times when they seemed to have been helpful and others when I have no idea if they were effective or not. I also took antipsychotic medication for a couple of years, sometimes alongside antidepressants, and other times on its own. A psychiatrist prescribed this type of medication for me to try to stabilize my moods and reduce suicidal thoughts. Although they seemed to balance my mood a bit, the side effects were debilitating, even on a low to medium dose. When I first started this medication, I woke up so drowsy that I could barely dress myself. Even when I prepared my clothes the night before, getting the right item of clothing onto the correct body part felt like a complicated sequence that my mind and body did not know how to perform. Luckily this drowsiness was limited to the early morning, and by the time I was at work I was okay.

On a small number of occasions, though, I woke up feeling so rough that I vomited, couldn't move around and had to call in sick. Even though antipsychotics seemed to help my mood, the side effects were too disruptive and detrimental to me.

Some people are very quick to judge people for taking

medication, and I feel this is very unjust. If medication is taken safely and it is helpful, then that's great. It has certainly helped me at some points in my life. It is always important to speak to a doctor about medication, follow the instructions and keep them in the loop about any side effects or changes experienced.

CHAPTER 7

DBT-Based Coping Techniques

Have you ever been having a hard time with your mental health and been told to do the following:

- Take a bubble bath?
- Take a walk?
- Do yoga?
- Journal?
- Drink herbal tea?
- Volunteer?

Whilst I love all of these things, and don't wish to discredit their usefulness for some people in certain situations, none of them has actually helped me when my BPD has been at its worst. In fact, these activities are actually liable to increase my distress levels and accelerate a crisis. Journalling about my fear when I am panicking only intensifies my terror. When I'm sad, having a bath reminds me of the New Year's Eve that I cried in the bath thinking about suicide. Going to a yoga class when I'm in distress is a bad idea too, because lying down on the mat makes me feel so out of control I struggle to get home.

Frustratingly, the coping tips and self-care strategies often found on health websites, in lifestyle magazines or information leaflets seem to be aimed at people with low to moderate depression and anxiety disorders. Public mental health campaigns rarely centre on people experiencing rapid mood changes, long-term suicidality, self-harm, psychosis or dissociation. This chapter puts coping techniques relevant to people with BPD 'front and centre'. These techniques are largely taken from DBT and require no or few resources, and they are free or low cost. It worth noting, though, that this chapter could never be a substitute for high-quality therapy with a skilled, qualified professional. That being said, I hope these pages can be helpful whilst you continue your search for support, are on a long waiting list or are seeking more tools alongside other support.

Why can using coping techniques be so hard?

Some people make using coping techniques sound so easy. Others forget that people with BPD can experience such high levels of distress that thinking clearly and processing information becomes almost impossible. I also had to learn that different coping techniques work for different times – when I am crying frantically I need something that will lower my level of emotion before I can begin to think clearly about my situation. When I started the process of using coping techniques and learning to be compassionate to myself, it also activated a lot of shame, guilt and sadness.

Before I start talking about coping techniques, I wanted

to acknowledge some of the reasons why a person might be reluctant to, or fearful of, using coping techniques:

- Thoughts of being undeserving of coping techniques.
- The belief that coping techniques are selfish, lazy or too self-indulgent.
- Past experience of using coping techniques that increased distress.
- Past experience of using coping techniques that were impossible to do during overwhelming distress.
- The belief that coping techniques don't work or are a waste of time.
- Thinking that coping techniques create the feeling of vulnerability or of being out of control.
- Fear of change that might happen if coping techniques are used.

There are three reminders that I used (and still use sometimes today) to get myself up and running with coping techniques when I didn't feel like doing them.

Everyone is worthy

Some people with BPD tend to think of themselves as less deserving of the comfort and kindness that they routinely give to others. It can feel so easy to show compassion to someone else and much harder to do it to yourself. My DBT therapist told me assertively that if I believed everyone deserves compassion, then that includes myself. It was a non-negotiable of my therapy; I could not have one rule for others and a different one for myself.

Act first

How was I supposed to treat myself with compassion if I didn't feel worthy? I told my therapist that using coping skills just felt wrong. She explained that I couldn't *make myself feel* worthy, but I could *act as if* I were worthy. This was a revelation to me because, prior to DBT, I had spent years trying to make myself 'feel worthy' enough of looking after myself. Instead, she taught me to act first, and then the emotion would follow.

Using coping techniques but not feeling worthy of them was initially strange and scary. However, repeatedly acting compassionately towards myself, even when I did not feel deserving, gradually made me feel worthy. After believing I had to change how I felt before I could change my actions, I was astonished to discover that the opposite was true.

Make it your own

Experiment with these coping techniques. Try them a number of times across a range of situations, days and moods. If a technique doesn't work once, that doesn't make it useless – it may work wonders in a different situation or when tweaked. It takes time to figure out which techniques work when and for which emotions.

The coping techniques I use are not set in stone, but change and grow with me (although I do have my favourites, of course!) Modify. Be flexible. Stay curious, and see what unfolds.

Understanding emotions

Amongst other functions, emotions make people act, assess

situations, stay safe, make decisions and communicate. Emotions are an essential component of developing social bonds, making yourself understood to others and finding meaning in life. They have many facets, from physical sensations, expressions and urges to behaving in certain ways.

Emotions can be prompted by events in the present moment that can be backed up with evidence: 'I am sad because I got my results letter and I didn't pass the exam.' Emotions can also be prompted by *interpretations* of events that cannot be backed up with evidence, but are instead based on past experiences: 'I am sad because my friend didn't reply to my text. That means she is ghosting me, just like the person I dated last month.' If you want to read more about the function of emotions, I recommend *DBT Skills Training Handouts and Worksheets* by Dr Marsha M. Linehan (2015).

Regardless of whether an emotion is prompted by an event or an interpretation of an event, they can be extremely powerful. They can cause intense physical sensations and create strong urges to act. Let's look now at DBT-based coping techniques that can help. For comprehensive information and worksheets about DBT and DBT skills, please refer to Linehan (2015).

Identifying emotions

Identifying emotions accurately is empowering. It is central to working out how to respond effectively. Here is a summary of my understanding of the nine key emotions that are commonly explored in DBT; for further information please refer to Linehan (2015).

Anger

- Triggers for anger include injustice, being threatened or having a goal blocked.
- Physical sensations include tense muscles, feeling hot, a racing heart and a feeling of pressure building.
- Urges include shouting, storming off, attacking or withdrawing.
- Fear can often be behind anger.

Sadness

- Triggers include the loss of someone or something precious, a death, illness, or something ending or not working out as you wanted.
- Physical sensations include tiredness and heaviness, which may be accompanied by crying. It can also be associated with difficulties concentrating, aches or numbness.
- Urges include crying, seeking comfort, slowing down, curling up, sleeping or withdrawing.

Fear

- Triggers include threat to life, health, reputation, relationships or something else that is valued.
- Physical sensations include a racing heart, sweating, breathlessness, tense muscles, nausea and stomach cramps and shaking.
- Fear can make people fight the threat, move away from it or freeze (become still, silent or dissociate).

**THE DIFFERENCE BETWEEN
FEAR AND ANXIETY**
Fear happens when the threat is very close. Anxiety occurs when a threat has become apparent, but is further away.

Joy

- Triggers include being connected to loved ones, receiving affection, being accepted or praised, things working out better than you expected and doing something enjoyable.
- It is characterized by laughing, smiling, high energy levels, bubbliness or lightness.
- Urges include wanting to share the joy with others, moving quickly, jumping up and down, talking a lot or expressing positive feelings.

Guilt

- Triggers include not acting in line with values, breaking a promise or causing someone to feel pain.
- It is associated with crying, feeling hot, looking at the floor and going red in the face.
- Urges include apologizing, confessing, asking for forgiveness, repairing damage or resolving to change.

Shame

- Triggers include being rejected by a valued group, being judged as inferior, mocked or betrayed.

- It is associated with looking at the floor, hiding, withdrawing from the rejecting group, over-apologizing or changing in an attempt to be accepted.
- Urges include hiding the thing that feels shameful or avoiding people who might judge us negatively.

Disgust

- Triggers include coming into contact with something dirty or contaminated, as well as being near someone you find immoral or witnessing cruelty.
- It is associated with nausea, gagging, feeling contaminated and repulsed.
- Urges include vomiting, grimacing, washing, looking away and casting judgement.

Envy

- Triggers include someone having something you need or want, as well as the success of a competitor.
- It is associated with longing, the loss of enjoyment and possibly satisfaction when a competitor experiences loss or failure.
- Urges include striving for the thing needed or desired and avoiding or disliking the envied person.

Jealousy

- This emotion happens when a loved person or object may be taken away by a rival.
- It is associated with suspicion, the desire to control and a racing heart.

- Urges include clinging, spying, accusing or threatening the rival, as well as self-improvement or showing off.

The easiest way for me to identify an emotion is to ask myself: 'What is my urge right now?' Urges usually pinpoint an emotion; for example, the urge to hide often reveals shame and the urge to run generally reveals fear. Many people discern their emotions via noticing their body sensations: 'My fists are clenched and my heart is racing, so that is probably anger' or 'I feel heavy and cold, so perhaps I am sad.'

Emotions may come alone or in succession. Anxiety is commonly followed by sadness and fear is often followed by anger. If you are experiencing multiple emotions, identify them one by one, starting with the strongest. I know this can be tricky, so take your time and try to be patient with yourself.

Event or interpretation of an event?

Perhaps one of the most well known DBT skills is 'Check the Facts' (Linehan 2015, pp.285–286). This skill can be used to work out whether an emotion is based on an actual event that can be backed up with facts, or whether it is an interpretation of an event. Below is my own version of 'Check the Facts' and how I do it.

1. Imagine sitting in front of a screen watching a film re-play of what happened.
2. Pause the film. Like a detective, jot down what you see and hear. Note facts, not opinions, judgements or theories.
3. Examine your notes. Is there evidence to prove that the

event actually happened? If yes, go to 'Responding effectively' below.

4. If no, write down your interpretations of the events. Interpretations are usually opinions, judgements and theories about what happened.

5. Next write down alternative interpretations about what happened or note down: 'I don't know for sure.' Uncertainty can feel scary and that's okay. Go to 'Balance the emotion' or 'Validate yourself'.

Responding effectively

When an emotion is activated by an actual event that can be backed up by facts, it is important to respond to the emotion effectively and to honour its function. Here are some examples of effective responses that honour the emotion.

Anger
- Address injustice.
- Protest and defend.
- Do a physical activity (in a balanced way).
- Problem-solve.
- Do something creative or productive.

Sadness
- Seek comfort (in a balanced way).
- Rest.
- Allow tears to come if they come.
- Soothe the senses. Grab a soft blanket, drink hot tea, look at relaxing photos.

Fear

- Protect and defend from threats.
- Problem-solve staying safe.
- Move to a safe space.
- Get help.

Joy

- Do more of what makes you joyful.
- Stay close to the source of happiness.
- Share your joy with others.

Guilt

- Apologize.
- Accept the consequences.
- Accept that mistakes are part of life.
- Repair damage.
- Prevent future mistakes as much as possible.

Shame

- Apologize to people you offended and change to fit in.
- Move away from the rejecting group and find others who are accepting.
- Work to make certain values and behaviours more widely accepted.

Disgust

- Move away from the source of disgust.
- Wash and clean.
- Promote the things you believe need promoting.

Envy
- Work hard to gain the desired or needed thing.
- Avoid people who make you feel envious.
- Ask others to share what they have with you.

Jealousy
- Strengthen and protect the threatened relationship.
- Leave the threatened relationship.

Balance the emotion

When an emotion arises from an *interpretation*, it is rarely effective to respond in line with it. As interpretations are based on past experiences, memories, judgements or hypothetical thoughts about unknown futures, responding can cause confusion and problems.

It is vital to understand that emotions based on interpretations are not dishonourable, invalid, unimportant or shameful. They have just as much importance and validity as emotions arising from events that can be backed up with fact. Emotions based on interpretations can feel incredibly strong (as anyone who has ever had a nightmare or a flashback to a terrifying moment can attest).

Whilst emotions based on actual events demand effective responses, emotions based on interpretations need to be balanced out. Balancing emotions is not about discrediting, shunning or depriving yourself of the right to feel your emotions; rather, it is a way of ensuring that actions are not driven by interpretations and preventing confusions or additional stress. For further information on this topic, and to learn about a skill called 'Opposite Action' in detail, please see *DBT Skills Training Handouts and Worksheets* by Dr Marsha M. Linehan (2015, p.231). Below are nine key emotions and ways I balance them out when they are driven by my interpretations, rather than actual events.

Anger

- Speak kindly and softly.
- Move gently and slowly.
- Stop defending.
- Relax your posture.

Sadness

- Move around.
- Increase your activity level.
- Make a plan or work on a goal.
- Connect with someone.
- Watch a comedy.

Fear

- Approach the source of fear.
- Engage with the source of fear.
- Stop protecting and being wary.

Guilt

- Keep breaking the value that causes guilt.
- Do not apologize.
- Do not make amends or self-punish for perceived mistakes or wrongdoing.

Shame
- Do the thing that leads (or may lead) to rejection.
- Seek acceptance elsewhere.
- Make eye contact.
- Do not apologize or change.

Disgust
- Approach the source of disgust.
- Engage with the source of disgust.
- Stop washing and cleaning.
- Stop judging.

Envy
- Appreciate and share.
- Celebrate the present.
- Stop or pause chasing a goal.
- Support the source of envy.

Jealousy
- Stop controlling and defending.
- Practise relaxation.
- Stop attempts to self-improve.

Validate yourself

Many people with BPD have experienced a lot of invalidation: "Stop crying," "Don't be so sensitive." Needing validation is completely normal and part of being human. However, people who have been invalidated a lot in the past may seek a lot of validation now. I used to feel so ashamed of my hunger for validation, but now I realize it's natural to want enough of what I once didn't have.

Whilst I know it's okay to seek validation from others sometimes, I am aware that others are not always available or capable of providing infinite amounts of validation. There-fore, it has proven very helpful for me to be able to validate myself at any given moment. When my DBT therapist initially suggested that I learn the skill of self-validation, I didn't think I could ever master it. The very idea of it made me cringe. The first few times I tried, I felt embarrassed and self-loathing: 'Who do you think you are giving yourself validation? You don't deserve this.'

Regardless of these thoughts and how ashamed I felt, I continued my attempts. When the self-critical thoughts in-evitably arose, I told myself 'your emotions are valid', 'you deserve comfort', 'you are allowed to feel sad'. With practice over time, validating myself felt less uncomfortable and more natural. I learned how it soothes my emotions (both those based on events and interpretations). I understood how vali-dating my emotions helps me accept myself when I am hav-ing thoughts about suicide or self-harm, rather than turning against myself, which fuels my distress.

A SCRIPT FOR PRACTISING SELF-VALIDATION

Feel free to adapt this script and make it your own. Please be aware that for some people self-validation can activate feelings of loss relating to the times when validation was needed, but was missing. Please approach this script gently and take breaks if needed.

I am experiencing intense emotions right now and it's really painful. I know that my emotions can be incredibly strong and even agonizing. I know that my emotions can rise quickly and I can quickly feel very distressed. I am aware that some people feel more emotions more intensely than others, and that's okay. I have been through so much in life and at times it has been very hard for me to cope. I recognize how hurt I have been and acknowledge the pain I have been through.

When I am having intense emotions, it can be hard to think clearly. Just because I am distressed now, it doesn't mean that I have always been distressed and always will be. I know that emotions are like waves; they rise to a peak and then fall. I will wait until this storm passes. It always passes.

Although I may have powerful urges to act on my emotion, I have a choice in this matter. If my emotion is based on an actual event, I can act effectively. If it is based on an interpretation of an event, it is likely to be more helpful not to act on it. I have a choice. I recognize how distressed I am feeling right now and how intensely I am feeling. I deserve validation, safety, comfort, respect and care.

For more information on self-validation, please see *DBT Skills Training Handouts and Worksheets* (Linehan, 2015).

Notice without judging

Humans have a tendency to label people, things and experiences with judgements: 'good', 'bad', 'pretty', 'ugly', 'difficult', 'easy'. Whilst judgements can be effective for making quick decisions (sharks are dangerous, I will not jump off the boat), they can lead us to a conclusion about something before we have all the facts.

Being able to notice something without judging it can bring calmness and clarity to situations. It can help regulate emotions, make thoughts feel less overwhelming, prevent acting on impulse and make more informed decisions. The word 'mindfulness' is often applied to the activity of noticing without judgement. I am not going to use the word 'mindfulness' here, though, because I am aware that some people have negative connotations attached to this word for numerous reasons.

Things to notice without judging can be internal such as emotions, thoughts and bodily sensations. They can also be external such as sounds, smells, textures, temperature, tastes and sights in our environment or other people.

Internal things to notice:

- Breath moving in and out of the nose.
- The emotion of sadness.
- Racing thoughts.
- Heart beating fast.
- The thought 'I am worthless'.
- The urge to send an email.

External things to notice:

- The colours in the carpet.
- The smell of bread.
- The shape of the table.
- The texture of jeans.
- The coolness of the water.
- Someone said: "I am going home now."
- Someone is scratching their head.

Attaching judgements to observations makes them into value-laden evaluations: 'The carpet is a hideous colour', 'She said she is going home in a rude tone', 'My breathing is too fast', 'My urges are terrible'. Noticing without judging leaves multiple possibilities open and tends to steady emotions. By contrast, evaluations can intensify emotions, and lead to conclusions made without evidence and additional stress.

Noticing without judging can feel uncomfortable at times. Judgements offer the illusion of control and certainty ('That person is bad'), which can feel comforting. However, the comfort of a judgement is short-lived. Try noticing internal and external things without attaching judgements. When a judgement inevitably and naturally arises, just notice it: 'There's a judgement'. See how this can help with emotional regulation and how liberating it can feel. For much more in-depth information on mindfulness and how it can help regulate emotions, please see Linehan (2015), and Aguirre and Galen (2013).

SOS

DBT teaches a number of skills for people to use in times of crisis, including the use of very cold water or ice cubes to activate the 'dive response', paced breathing and paired muscle relaxation (Linehan 2015, pp.329–331). Personally, I don't use those skills; however, I do find the STOP skill very helpful for managing moments of overwhelming emotion and intense distress (Linehan 2015, p.327). I have made my own slightly simplified version of 'STOP', which I call 'SOS'. SOS stands for 'Stop, Observe, Slow down'. It helps me when I feel distressed, frantic and at risk of acting on urges that will only make things more difficult for me.

1. Stop: When emotions and urges to act are rising, visualize a 'STOP' sign in your mind. This is your signal to pause. Lie down, sit or stand still (depending on where you are), and do not move for at least a minute. Count to 60. Repeat as needed.

2. Observe: Notice emotions, thoughts, urges and physical sensations without judgement. Put your observations into words: 'I am having the emotion of shame. My thoughts are racing. I am thinking about being rejected. My heart is beating fast. My palms are sweaty. I am having the urge to run home.'

3. Slow down: Before moving, make a careful plan for the next few minutes or hours. Don't think too far into the future. Will acting this way be effective? Is it in line with your values? Will you look back tomorrow and be okay with how you handled this situation? Only move when

you are confident that you can proceed effectively, not frantically. Move slowly. If you are not slow yet, return to step 1.

The trickiest part of SOS for me is daring to use it in moments of agony and agitation. Sometimes SOS is the last thing I feel like doing when I am in distress, and there are times when I don't manage to use it. There will be slip-ups when learning this technique and beyond, but that's okay. It takes practice and it's tricky to get things right all the time. However, if you are trying this skill, it is not lessening your distress and you feel you need urgent support to keep yourself safe, please contact emergency services immediately.

Worst possible outcome...and coping

When I'm fearful or anxious about something, my thoughts usually turn to the worst possible outcome. Trying to stop thinking about situations that scare me only makes me think about them more. One therapist illustrated this point by asking me not to think of a pink elephant. Of course, this made a pink elephant immediately appear in my mind.

In DBT, I learned a skill known as 'Cope Ahead', which, strangely enough, invites detailed thinking about the worst possible outcome for a limited time (Linehan 2015, p.256). However, there is a twist: it involves thinking about the worst possible outcome *and* coping. As this skill can be emotionally challenging, it is recommended to do it when you are feeling fairly relaxed and taking time afterwards to do something soothing, like watching a favourite comedy or going for a calming walk.

1. Set a timer for 5 minutes. Now imagine as vividly as possible what the worst possible outcome would be like. Think about the sounds, smells, sights and feelings with as much detail as possible. How would it feel emotionally and physically to go through that?

2. Once 5 minutes has finished, set the timer again for another 5 minutes. Now imagine coping with this worst possible outcome. What would coping look like? How would you respond? What would you say and do? Imagine the emotions, thoughts and physical sensations associated with coping with as much detail as possible. If it helps, write it down or draw a picture. Once you have finished, it is time to soothe yourself and do a calming activity.

Fear usually has two layers. The first layer is the situation itself and the second is the ability to cope. This technique breaks down the second layer by increasing thoughts of coping, rather than being completely destroyed should the worst possible outcome happen. Using this technique has led to a decrease in the amount of time I spend thinking about situations that frighten me.

Meet in the middle

When life feels overwhelming or uncertain, some people gravitate towards behaving in extremes in an attempt to feel more in control. When I was younger and anxious about my exams, I would study for so long that it made me exhausted and unwell. Some people go to the opposite extreme when feeling worried about exams and do not study at all.

There have also been times when I've not cared for myself at all and spent every last drop of energy helping others.

'All-or-nothing thinking' is usually behind acting in extreme ways. All-or-nothing thoughts often contain the following words:

- Must ('I *must* make everyone happy').
- Always ('I *always* embarrass myself').
- Never ('She *never* listens to me').

Try to notice instances of all-or-nothing thinking: 'I am having the thought that I should never skip cleaning my kitchen'. See if some flexibility can be added to the thought: 'Maybe I can skip cleaning today and catch up with it tomorrow instead?' I often have the thought 'I must never annoy anyone', yet the rigidity of this thought sets such a high standard that I am constantly scanning people's faces for signs of irritation.

There is a module in DBT called 'Middle Path', which is about finding a 'Synthesis between Opposites' (Linehan 2015, p.74). Put simply, this means balancing two ideas that can be opposite to, or in conflict with, one another. Examples of opposites or competing elements to balance include: resting with being active, caring for others with caring for yourself, self-indulgence with self-denial. I think of balancing opposites as meeting in the middle. It also refers to the idea that two things can be true at the same time; for example, I can be hardworking and still have a rest, or I can be kind to others and still care for myself. Here are some examples of synthesizing dialectics:

- Meeting a friend for a short time instead of cancelling completely.
- Sending a couple of messages instead of many or none at all.
- Campaigning for something you believe in, but occasionally having a break.
- Asking for help now and again instead of trying to manage alone.
- Leaving a tiny smudge in your make-up instead of removing it all and starting again.

Initially, the idea of meeting in the middle and balancing opposites made me feel out of control – I feared I would become half-hearted, lazy, selfish or not as successful. The only thing that happened, though, was a decrease in my stress levels and an increased sense of wellbeing. Synthesizing dialectics actually freed up my time and space for responding to my needs as and when they arose. In turn, this enabled me to use more coping techniques. I hope you will be able to explore meeting in the middle or balancing opposites yourself too, and seeing what positives it brings to your life.

The DBT-based coping techniques outlined here are just a handful (albeit a carefully chosen one!) of the huge range out there. Feel free to explore others more widely and in more depth using the 'Resources' listed at the end of the book. I hope that the techniques in this book and any others you encounter can bring you comfort. Whether you are fatigued from having intense emotions, frustrated by difficulties accessing support or in a moment of panic, I hope they can bring comfort, confidence and calm.

CHAPTER 8

Self-Harm and Suicide

What is self-harm?

Self-harm is often described in books and on websites as someone hurting themselves as a way of coping with difficult feelings. Whilst it is true that people self-harm in order to try to manage emotional pain, I want to break it down a bit more. A 2016 review of a number of studies by Edmondson, Brennan and House showed that people might self-harm for the following reasons:

- To temporarily regulate emotions and relieve distress.
- As a distraction from emotional pain and to focus on something else.
- To make 'invisible' emotional pain 'visible' on the body.
- As a self-punishment.
- To manage dissociation.
- To create sensations.
- To deal with the risk of suicide.

I have come to understand self-harm as something someone does to get their needs met when there are no other options available. As I will explore throughout this chapter, this could be the need for emotional regulation, validation, acceptance, expression, comfort or safety.

Research highlights a number of potential risk factors for self-harm, including 'a history of child maltreatment and stressful life experiences' (Cipriano, Cella and Cotrufo 2017). LGBTQ+ people are also are at higher risk of self-harm, most likely due to experiences of abuse, discrimination and harassment (Williams *et al.* 2019).

Prejudice and discrimination of all kinds are likely to be risk factors for self-harm, although much more detailed research needs to be done on this topic. Without a doubt, more needs to be done to address health inequalities and to ensure the wellbeing of all groups in society, not just those with the most power.

My experience of self-harm

I started self-harming before I hit 10 years old. I was sensitive to everything and anything; I didn't know how to cope with how I felt. The most frequent reason I self-harmed was because I believed I had upset others, and I hoped that hurting myself would make me a 'better person'. The other main reason I self-harmed as a child was to control my anger. At times, my rage was so strong that if I didn't hurt myself, I would scream and shout until I was breathless and hoarse. Because my yelling upset everyone around me, which made me feel even more ashamed of myself, hurting myself seemed like the better option.

I continued to self-harm to varying degrees throughout childhood, adolescence and early adulthood, until I started DBT. Whilst anger was no longer a problem once I became an adult, I still didn't know how to manage my intense feelings of shame without hurting myself. Furthermore, when people treated me disrespectfully or cruelly (which, unfortunately, some people did), I felt deserving of this poor treatment. After all, wasn't I too emotional, too sensitive, too expressive, too fragile and too excitable to be lovable? On the rare occasions that I felt I deserved to be treated with more respect, I punished myself for not knowing how to walk away.

All in all, self-harm was the only tool I had back then for preventing outbursts of emotion. If someone said something that made me want to fall to the floor sobbing, I could simply say "I just need to use the bathroom." There I could hurt myself until my emotions drained out. I could then emerge from the cubicle smiling, wash my hands and return to whatever I was doing. Over the years, hurting my body when my mind was in agony has allowed me to function. On a road trip with friends, one comment upset me so much that if I hadn't hurt myself secretly in the back of the car, I think I may have jumped out into the road. On a backpacking trip, it stopped me from leaving remote hostels in the middle of the night. When I haven't known other ways of coping with emotion that feels unbearable, I have turned to self-harm for a moment of relief. Of course, as quickly as the relief came it disappeared, only to be replaced with more anxiety, guilt, shame or sadness.

Stopping self-harm

I tried to stop self-harming on multiple occasions, but the

advice I read online or in books didn't seem to work for me. Techniques to stop self-harming usually involve finding 'alternatives', such as holding ice cubes, snapping an elastic band on the wrist, drawing on skin with a marker and practising relaxation techniques. The problem I found with these alternatives is that they never were *true* alternatives. If I wanted to self-harm in order to punish myself, then snapping an elastic band on my wrist just felt like a bit of a joke. When I wanted to hurt myself in order to stop myself sobbing in front of my friends, going into the bathroom and drawing on myself didn't work. Moreover, the fact that these alternatives didn't work for me made me feel more hopeless.

Once I started DBT, though, I realized that I needed a different approach. The first step towards hurting myself less was to identify what need my self-harm was trying to meet. Recognizing the need accurately enabled me to look for a true 'alternative', or, if there was no accurate replacement, to find a completely different strategy for meeting that need. How did I do this, though? I used a number of the techniques explained in Chapter 7. First, I used the SOS technique to slow myself down. Second, I identified my emotion and then checked the facts (also explained in Chapter 7). If my emotion is activated by something that can be backed up with evidence, I respond accordingly. If my emotion is based on an interpretation, then I use self-validation or balance the emotion (or both!).

It is often helpful to notice thoughts, emotions, physical sensations and urges without judging them – acknowledge how strong and all-consuming they feel. By noticing without judgement, their power may lessen. Avoid labels like 'bad', 'shameful', 'ridiculous', 'weak', 'a failure' or any other self-judgements. If you find that challenging, notice this desire to judge and criticize. If it helps, imagine someone is sitting nearby offering support – a loved one, a book character or even a pet. Visualize them helping you through this moment in the way you would like to be supported. What would they say?

IS SELF-HARM ADDICTIVE?

When the body is hurt, the brain releases chemicals called endorphins (natural opiates) that alleviate pain, release stress and that can create positive feelings. There is some research to suggest that the release of endorphins can play a role in why some people self-harm (Sandman and Kemp 2011). Some studies show that people who self-harm may get used to the effects of endorphins, making it harder to stop (Sandman and Kemp 2011).

As challenging as it may be to stop self-harming, it is more than achievable. Identifying the needs behind self-harm and then gently exploring new ways of getting these needs met can be a helpful starting point. Please know that self-harming is nothing to be ashamed of. Use the 'Resources' at the end of this book if you need help.

The needs behind self-harm
Emotional regulation
Sometimes emotions are so intense that they feel unbearably

painful. It is as if their intensity creates so much pressure that containing them feels impossible. As a result, some people self-harm to 'release' this pressure and relieve discomfort or pain. Some describe self-harm as having a calming effect that quietens upsetting thoughts. By contrast, some people experience feelings of numbness or emptiness, which can be unsettling or distressing. Causing physical harm to the body can create physical sensations and generate emotions that make some people feel more 'alive'.

Some people find that scribbling on paper or making marks with paint, engaging with music or another creative activity allows emotions to 'flow out' when they feel 'too much' or 'flow in' when they feel empty of feeling. When I'm emotionally dysregulated, I sometimes set an alarm and nap for 20 minutes if I can. I usually find this rebalances my emotions a little. Eating in a balanced way is also helpful for stabilizing my mood, which is why I always carry snacks!

Validation

Some people self-harm as a way of making invisible emotional pain visible on the body. If words are not available for distress or there is nobody there to listen, hurting the body can be a means of communication. This communication is usually individuals communicating with themselves, although sometimes it could be an attempt to communicate with others. As I will explain further below, it is a misconception that people self-harm 'for attention'. A lot of people who self-harm do it privately without others knowing. Many individuals don't talk about it for fear of judgement or 'bothering' others.

Throughout my teenage years, I worried that my emotional pain was 'made up' and, at times, hurting my body acted as 'proof' that my distress was real. Although it was a secret, part of me wished that someone had known and had been able to help me. Sometimes people self-harm because caring for their injuries acts as a substitute for the compassion and tenderness that they need. The self-validation script that I shared in Chapter 7 can be helpful in these instances. Acknowledging your own emotions (even whilst longing for validation from someone else) can be soothing. It can be helpful to watch or read about others' experiences online or in books (take care to avoid stigmatizing content, though).

It may also be worth seeking online or in-person spaces to safely express thoughts and emotions. This could be a listening helpline, an online support forum, a therapy group or community support groups. If a space doesn't make you feel safe or welcome, it is important to leave straight away.

Control

Self-harm can create the feeling of being in control after traumatic or difficult experiences (Klonsky 2009). Sometimes people who feel trapped, powerless or out of control may self-harm in order to retain a sense of autonomy over their body, life or circumstances. At times, self-harm can become a 'ritual' involving repetitive behaviours and a routine that creates a sense of predictability and familiarity. For some people, hurting the body can feel like a way to 'start over again' after doing something 'wrong' or to 'wash away' their 'mistakes'. In the past, I self-harmed because I believed hurting myself would give me more self-control and make me behave 'better'.

Stopping dissociation

Research highlights that many people self-harm as a way to stop dissociating when things are traumatic or overwhelming. This is because physical pain can make people feel more connected to their body or bring them into the present moment once again. Self-harm can also be used as a distraction from intrusive thoughts or to curtail flashbacks. A small percentage of people self-harm in order to prevent suicidal actions (the second part of this chapter is about suicide and how to manage feeling suicidal).

Grounding techniques can anchor the body and mind to the present moment and surroundings. This can steady the flashbacks, dissociation, intrusive thoughts or painful memories that lead to urges to self-harm. Some people find holding ice or running their hands under very cold water effective ways of grounding themselves. Others find particular smells helpful, such as very bitter coffee or a strong perfume.

SOME GROUNDING TECHNIQUES

A grounding technique that I learned in my DBT group involves tracing around your hand with a finger from the opposite hand. Breathe in as you move your finger up and breathe out as you move your finger down. Keep going until you feel yourself connecting with your body, surroundings and the present moment. It sounds trivial, but it can be very effective.

Another well-known grounding strategy is known as the '5, 4, 3, 2, 1' technique. Do this by looking for five things you can see, four things you can feel, three things you can hear, two you can smell and one you can taste. You don't have to be somewhere with a lot going on to do this – you have the feel of your breath, the ground beneath your feet, the weight of your arms and so on.

Myths about self-harm

Self-harm is often misunderstood by the public and health professionals, as well as misrepresented in the media. I wanted to shed light on some of the most common myths surrounding self-harm.

Myth #1: People who self-harm are attention seekers

People who self-harm are experiencing emotional distress or a difficulty of some kind. Seeking support, connection or validation is not the same as being an attention seeker. The term 'attention seeker' is judgemental and shows no understanding or compassion for people in pain.

Myth #2: Only girls and women self-harm

People of all genders can experience self-harm – there is no single specific gender that self-harms. Some studies show that females are more likely to self-harm than men, whereas others show no difference in the rate of self-harm between cis-gender females and cis-gender males.

However, research has consistently shown high rates of self-harm amongst transgender, non-binary or gender-variant people. A study of trans mental health and wellbeing by the Scottish Trans Alliance found that 53 per cent of trans people had self-harmed, with 11 per cent currently self-harming (Mc-Neil *et al.* 2012). Many trans, non-binary and gender-variant people continue to experience high levels of verbal abuse, harassment and violence, all of which can be hugely detrimental to mental health.

Myth #3: Self-harm is a 'phase' that people 'grow out' of

Many people think that only young people self-harm. Whilst some studies show that it is more common in young people, individuals of all ages can self-harm, including those who are older. Viewing self-harm as a 'phase' that people 'grow out' of is inaccurate, as well as irresponsible because it dismisses the pain that someone is going through. Whilst some people self-harm many times, others do it only once or during a short period of difficulty.

Myth #4: Self-harm always involves cutting

If a person is hurting their body in response to emotional distress of some kind, then it is self-harm. Self-harm takes many forms, and no type is more deserving of help than another.

What is suicide and why do people feel suicidal?

Suicide is when a person intentionally ends their own life. There are many reasons that might cause a person to think about suicide, have 'suicidal thoughts' or 'feel suicidal'. Difficult experiences or traumatic events, such as abuse, bullying, bereavement, rejection, financial problems or relationship breakdowns, can lead a person to think about suicide. Some people who think about suicide have a mental health condition, whilst others do not. Chances are, if you are diagnosed with BPD, you will probably have felt suicidal at some point or other. You are most definitely not alone in this experience.

Suicidal thoughts and feeling suicidal varies from person to person; there is no one set experience. However, common feelings associated with feeling suicidal are despair, help-lessness, powerlessness or hopelessness. Suicidal thoughts can be 'intrusive', unwanted thoughts or images that appear in the mind, and can be distressing for many (but not all) people. Sometimes people who have suicidal thoughts believe they are completely worthless and that everything in life is pointless. Some people think about suicide because they feel so much pain (emotional, physical or both) that dying seems preferable to being alive. Not all people who have suicidal thoughts want to die, though. For me, suicidal thoughts have always been a response to feeling overwhelming emotional pain and desperately wanting it to stop, rather than a desire for my life to end.

Who feels suicidal?

Anyone can feel suicidal regardless of gender, ethnicity, nationality, sexuality, socioeconomic or educational back-ground. A person can feel suicidal no matter what their bank balance, address, how loved they are, how many friends they have or what they do all day. Stonewall's *LGBT in Britain – Health* report states that 'one in eight LGBT people aged 18–24 (13 per cent) said they've attempted to take their own life in the last year' (Bachmann and Gooch 2018, p.5). The same report showed that 'almost half of trans people (46 per cent) have thought about taking their own life in the last year' (p.5).

So much more work needs to be done to ensure the safety and wellbeing of LGBTQ+ people.

My experience of suicidal thoughts

For around a decade, I thought about suicide as much as I thought about what to eat, wear or watch on TV. Suicidal thoughts were such a large part of my life that entire places, songs, brands and photographs are overlain with the memory of feeling suicidal. There are certain streets that I can't walk down without remembering myself crying desperately. There's also a particular TV theme tune that I can't listen to because it reminds me of watching TV feeling suicidal, but pretending to be fine.

I feel equal amounts of sadness for enduring pain for so long and delight that I stayed alive to experience today. Above all, though, my thoughts of suicide were confusing because they felt at odds with the love I felt for my family, friends, the world around me and the joy I felt for everything in it. I guess that's the thing I didn't know then about feeling suicidal. It doesn't matter how much love you have for life or how loved you are, suicidal thoughts can still follow you around like ghosts.

Since I completed DBT and started living a calmer life with my partner and our dog, I have rarely felt suicidal. This is because I rarely experience the agony I used to and, when I do, I know how to bear the pain so it doesn't consume me. These days, if suicidal thoughts arise, they are fleeting visitors. I thank them for reminding me of everything I overcame, my sensitivity and for nudging me to rest.

What to do if you are having suicidal thoughts
Talk to a person or an organization that you trust
This could be a friend, family member or a professional such as a therapist, doctor, support worker or teacher. It could also be an organization that supports people in emotional distress such as a healthcare organization, certain charities or helplines (I have included a list of helpful resources at the end of this book for you to check out). It is worth noting that different organizations have varying levels of confidentiality when supporting people who feel suicidal.

Keep professionals in the loop
It is really important to keep any therapists or doctors up to date about how you're feeling, especially if you (or others around you) have noticed a change. They may be able to tweak something in your treatment to help.

Remove anything that could be used to hurt yourself
Hide, lock away or dispose of anything you could use to hurt yourself, or ask someone else to help you do this. Even if you keep something and know where to find it, put it somewhere that takes time and energy to reach. Wrapping things in extra-strong sticky tape or freezing items in blocks of ice can also prevent grabbing things during times of distress.

Go to a place that makes you feel safer
Consider going to a place that makes you feel safer. When I have been suicidal, I have usually felt safer sitting in a café or a library than being at home alone. The attention I can

give to my surroundings helps me feel more grounded and connected to the world.

Use the coping techniques outlined in Chapter 7
The SOS technique 'noticing without judging' can be particularly relevant when feeling suicidal.

Contact emergency services
If your life is in immediate danger, or if you don't know where to turn for the help you need, contact emergency services. Although suicide feels like an option now, your future self is going to thank you for staying alive more than you know right now.

Talking about suicidal thoughts
In the past, I have been ridiculed, insulted and even screamed at when telling people about my suicidal thoughts. I know how much it hurts to feel suicidal and to talk about it, only to be blanked, invalidated or shamed.

The 'cheer up' response
The 'cheer up' response involves being told that I 'shouldn't' be suicidal because of all the good things I have in my life. All this does is deepen the guilt I feel for having suicidal thoughts and increases their intensity. Plus, anyone who knows me understands that my optimistic outlook is just part of who I am and has nothing to do with my suicidal thoughts.

The 'let's talk about something else' response
This response involves changing the subject to anything

else: "Your hair looks nice," "Lovely weather," "What shall we have for dinner?" etc. It also involves phrases that draw an invisible line under the conversation such as "Let's talk about something more cheerful" or "Let's not dwell on this."

I can't help but feel completely mortified when people respond to me in this way when I try to talk about feeling suicidal. The fact that I told someone something so personal and they either weren't able to (or didn't want to) listen makes me feel like I stripped naked in an important work meeting.

At times, it might have looked like I didn't understand when someone couldn't, or didn't want to, engage with me about suicidal thoughts, but really, I do. I know that everyone has their boundaries and their own life going on. Years have passed and still I feel embarrassed about the discomfort I have caused others in the past by sharing my suicidal thoughts with them. I never wanted to 'bother' people. I never spoke flippantly. If I talked to someone, it's because I was trying – really trying – to stay alive.

If you are living in secrecy, silence or judgement for having suicidal thoughts, please keep searching for the people who will give you empathy. They are out there, even though it may take time and patience to find them. Use the 'Resources' at the end of this book, and follow up all leads with every ounce of creativity and determination. Please don't give up.

Staying in hospital

Some people with BPD might be admitted to a mental health hospital for a time if there is no other way to stay safe. People who stay in hospital are known as 'inpatients', as opposed to 'outpatients', who attend hospital during the day only. Some inpatients are 'voluntary' (or 'informal') patients, which means that they should have the right to come and go within the hospital. Others are 'involuntary' (or 'formal') patients, which means that mental health professionals have decided that they must be admitted to hospital for safety reasons.

When professionals decide that a person must be hospitalized, possibly without their consent, this is known as 'being sectioned'. Involuntary patients who have been sectioned may be stopped from leaving the hospital and given treatment, even if they do not agree to it. People who are sectioned have certain legal rights depending on their country or state, as well as depending on their specific type of section. According to Mind, people who are sectioned and detained in hospital in the UK have the right to get information leaflets about being sectioned when they arrive on the ward, they can appeal against their section to a mental health tribunal, see their sectioning papers, have a meeting with hospital managers and get help from an independent mental health advocate (IMHA), amongst other rights. I recommend looking at Mind's website for the most up-to-date advice, or looking at an equivalent source of information for your country or state. It always makes sense to be prepared with knowledge about your legal rights.

Hospital stays may involve assessments, medical treatments, therapy and activities such as exercise or art. However, like all types of mental healthcare, the quality varies dramatically between services. This means that some people have helpful and positive hospital stays, whilst others have stays that are counterproductive, invalidating or even traumatic.

A message of hope

I never dreamed that my life could ever become as calm and happy as it is now. If you are reading this whilst thinking about suicide, I want you to know that things can change more than you are able to imagine right now. I have thought about suicide thousands of times, and today I am incredibly grateful that I gave myself the chance to see how things would turn out. Please don't deny yourself the chance to see how things will turn out for you.

When I have been at my most suicidal, thinking about my loved ones actually made me more distressed. In these moments, I felt so unworthy of love that it hurt to hold these people in my mind. At these times, I found non-human things easier to hold on to – the idea of reading a book, drinking coffee, going to the beach and watching a travel documentary were some of my reasons to stay. Drawing a picture, making a card or writing a poem has also helped me cling on when I thought I might let go.

So often, people with BPD who are thinking of suicide believe that they are unlovable, unworthy of care or don't deserve to live. Sometimes, life feels too painful to bear, and it seems like the agony will last forever. Please know that present feelings do not predict future ones. Contact a helpline. Research local support groups or charities. Use the 'Resources' at the end of this book. Keep asking for help from professionals, even if you have been turned away 20 times already. Everyone deserves support and that includes you.

So many people who previously considered or tried ending their lives have gone on to find more meaning than ever imagined. Many go on to help others. If I had acted on my thoughts of suicide, I would not be here writing this book, which I hope you will find supportive and comforting. Please know that I have had sleepless nights not knowing if I could make it until morning; I no longer have such nights. Things can change more than you can dream of right now.

CHAPTER 9

Calmer, Happier Relationships

For years, the myth that people with BPD are incapable of having strong, happy relationships made me doubt both my future and my value as a person. Yet relationships are – and have always been – my richest source of joy and fulfilment. I am lucky to have the most generous and kind-hearted family, a handful of very close friends and an incredibly thoughtful partner, all of whom bring me love, meaning, solace and fun. Meeting my partner in 2017 was like coming to shore after being at sea. His values and outlook mapped almost identically onto mine, and his steadfast personality complemented my excitability.

In my early twenties, I experienced many painful, and even abusive, experiences in the context of romantic relationships. These traumatic experiences left my confidence more in tatters than I initially released. After reflecting on how hurt I had been, I knew I could only be in a relationship with someone who could – without exception – validate my emotions and celebrate my sensitivity. When I began dating again, I vowed to myself that anyone who treated me disrespectfully or abusively would get no second chances. I am happy to say I honoured this promise.

It is a cruel irony, though, that my relationships are the most valuable aspect of my life and the starting point for almost all of my anxieties. If I was scared of losing something less important than my relationships, then maybe I wouldn't feel so distressed? The good news, however, is that there are things that can help manage and reduce these fears. Although the therapies outlined in Chapter 5 can be very helpful for anxiety relating to relationships, I know that unfortunately not everyone has easy access to these treatments at all times. This chapter aims to offer support to anyone who, like me, often fears abandonment. It shares insights from my own learning on managing anxieties in relationships, starting off with relationships in general and then moving on to romantic relationships more specifically. If you are looking to manage anxiety and develop closer, more rewarding relationships, I hope the next few pages can be a guide for you.

Hypervigilance

Since I was about 14, there are some people in whose presence I have never or rarely relaxed. In school there were certain teachers who would make me sweat relentlessly, not because I was intimidated by their questions or had a crush on them, but because I felt like they were looking straight through me and they could see my mental health problems. Part of me was terrified of being approached and questioned, whilst another part of me longed for this to happen in case they could help.

Some of my friendships in adolescence and young adulthood, too, have been marked by constant anxiety. The closer I became to some friends, the more embarrassment and self-loathing I felt. Have I said too much? Will I scare them? Will I overwhelm them? Am I inappropriate? Did I make them uncomfortable? Am I unbearable? The same anxiety happened in romantic relationships too, but even more intensely. I have been, and sometimes still am, extremely aware of where people are and where they are looking. I spend a lot of time anticipating when a person might move or speak or what they may be thinking. The state of being highly alert for any signs of danger and anticipating threats even where there are none is known as 'hypervigilance'.

People who have experienced trauma or other difficult emotional experiences often find themselves being hypervigilant. People who are hypervigilant may feel 'on guard' or 'on high alert' a lot of the time. Hypervigilance is associated with a racing heart, sweating, a high startle response and difficulties with sleeping or relaxing. I often find myself scanning others' faces for signs of annoyance, checking my phone after sending messages to see if people have replied and being overly aware of where people are physically in relation to me. I also startle very, very easily.

When I lived in a house share with good friends, I was in a constant state of hypervigilance. I could not relax properly, even when I was chilling in my room, because I was overly aware of my friends' movements around the house, their facial expressions and body language. I didn't know how to manage the part of my brain that feared their rejection and scanned for danger. Once, when I returned home from a fun camping holiday with my friends, I had a huge breakdown in my bedroom. Although I had loved bike riding, going to the beach and playing games round the campfire with them, I had been in a state of hypervigilance for four days during the trip. With nothing between my friends and I but the nylon tent sheet, my level of hypervigilance ate me alive.

Thankfully, when I moved in with my partner, hypervigilance in my own home stopped. It was like getting out of an ocean into a still pool. I find it much easier to manage being around one person than multiple people, and also my partner's presence calms me right down. I have never been able to relax so much around anyone as him. I realize now that spending time alone, or with someone I can relax completely with, like my partner, is essential for my emotional regulation.

When I was a teenager and a younger adult, I pushed myself to the limit by staying out for a long time with friends and going to social events when I was already exhausted. Nowadays, I work with my anxiety levels, rather than against them. I schedule my days precisely to balance time with others with time by myself. Additionally, I refuse to feel guilty if I need to leave an event early. Doing yoga, painting, reading, taking hot showers and listening to audiobooks calm my hypervigilance. I recommend exploring different activities to see which ones might bring you some moments of peace. Here are my tips for this:

- Find a diary or a calendar in a format that works for you. Experiment with different sizes, from pocket-size to A4, a diary app on your phone, a calendar on your computer or traditional pen and paper. It doesn't need to be fancy – it can even be the back of a used envelope with squares drawn on it for each day of the week. I use A4 size diaries because I like a lot of space to plan in detail. I normally get one with high-quality paper so my highlighters and felt-pens don't bleed through.

- Map out your week and/or month on your calendar. First, write in the essentials, like work or volunteering, if applicable to you, caring responsibilities if you have children or other people to care for, and any appointments. People with mental health problems often have several appointments to attend or medication to collect, so writing these in too will be helpful.

- It might seem over the top, but schedule time for cleaning, cooking, looking after pets, travelling and any other things you do. Whilst writing this book, I had to plot chunks of time for writing and editing. It might look fussy to schedule every little thing, but for me it has brought comfort and a sense of ease. Without seeing my day, week and month visually, I feel like I don't have time for all the things I need and want to do. When I see my time sectioned into chunks, I feel more confident that I do have time and I can cope with all my demands.

- This next step is very important, even though you may be tempted to skip it. *Schedule in time for yourself.* By writing this in, you are making time for yourself a commitment, not an optional extra. I even write things in that don't involve other people or require leaving the house, like 'watch TV' and 'read'.

Unravelling self from others

As discussed in Chapter 2, emotional changes in people with BPD usually happen in response to interpersonal situations. Sudden shifts in mood can be triggered by what someone says or does, especially in close or valued relationships. When I feel intense shame, fear or sadness, it is almost certainly in response to the behaviour of someone I care about (such as a friend) or someone who has authority in my life (for example, a manager at work).

Interpersonal situations that have activated, or still activate, strong emotional responses in me sometimes include:

- A partner asking me to talk to them later because they are currently busy.
- A friend not returning my calls or texts.
- A colleague giving me feedback.
- A friend telling me they need space.
- A doctor telling me about a problem and how to improve it.

These situations can trigger a downward spiral in my mood because I often evaluate myself as a 'bad person' or as having done something 'wrong'. I jump to the conclusion that my actions have caused others to feel upset or angry or that they now disapprove of me. I then predict that this person is going to either criticize or reject me because they have seen what an 'awful' person I really am. Reading about the development of BPD (see Chapter 3) can be comforting and bring an understanding of why people with this condition tend to find criticism difficult.

Cognitive distortions

Learning about 'cognitive distortions' has helped me to manage the interpersonal situations that often activate shame, fear or sadness in me. Cognitive distortions, also known as 'thinking errors', are inaccurate or biased ways of thinking that stop people from understanding themselves, others and situations accurately. When my mood spirals in response to something that happens in my relationships, I am usually experiencing one or more of these cognitive distortions.

All-or-nothing thinking

All-or-nothing thinking is thinking in extremes and seeing situations, others or ourselves as 'completely good' or 'completely bad' rather than a blend of positives and negatives. This cognitive distortion is sometimes called 'black and white thinking' because the 'shades of grey' in the middle are either forgotten or disregarded. Whilst it momentarily creates the illusion of certainty and simplicity, it stops a person seeing things as they really are. Notice when you are thinking in an all-or-nothing manner, and write down the middle ground you may have forgotten or overlooked. Challenging this kind of thinking might feel scary at first, so be sure to use self-validation (see Chapter 7).

Mind reading

Mind reading is jumping to conclusions about what others are thinking. Imagine that you are having a conversation with someone you know and they yawn. Mind reading would be to assume that they are bored of talking with you instead of being open to other possibilities, such as their dog or baby having woken them in the night or the fact that they may be exhausted from working hard all week. I have a tendency to mind read and, quite frequently, I 'feel certain' that someone is judging me negatively. However, 'feeling certain' is not the same as having factual evidence, so I am working on noticing when I am mind reading and checking the facts (see Chapter 7).

Emotional reasoning

Emotional reasoning is using emotions as 'evidence' that something is true. When I'm home alone at night, sometimes I have the thought that someone might be in my garden planning to break into my house. I feel frightened and my heart starts racing, and then – before I know it – I am using my fear as 'proof' that there *really* is someone in the garden. Although emotions give us important information, they cannot reliably be used as evidence that our thoughts are true. Other examples of emotional reasoning include 'I feel sad, which means I truly have lost my friend forever' or 'I feel guilty, so I really must have done something wrong'. Checking the facts is an effective way of challenging emotional reasoning. Whilst I usually find that it doesn't remove my emotion, it shows me that I don't need to act on it.

Catastrophic thinking

Catastrophic thinking is thinking that the worst-case scenario is going to happen. I engage in catastrophic thinking from time to time, especially when I'm under stress. Recently, I made a completely honest mistake. I started thinking catastrophically and worried that people would think I was dishonest and I would be disgraced. Of course, this didn't happen.

On some level, I believe that catastrophic thinking helps me cope with the worst. In actual fact, this cognitive distortion robs me of the opportunity to be calm, as none of my imagined catastrophes has actually happened. Using the 'worst possible outcome...and coping' technique or checking the facts (both outlined in Chapter 7) often helps me interrupt catastrophic thinking.

Personalizing

Personalizing is thinking that something is your fault or your responsibility even when it's not. When someone is sad, my first thought is 'What did I say to hurt them?' I try to notice my tendency to blame myself and then look for other possibilities. Everyone has things going on in their life that may not be about you. Whilst I may think I have upset a friend if they don't reply to my message, I try to remain open to the possibility that they may be busy doing something, not in the mood to text right now, working or asleep.

Personalizing can range from mild to extremely serious. In my early twenties, I blamed myself for the abuse I suffered from others. I felt safer blaming myself for the abuse than holding others accountable for their maltreatment. Self-blame gave me the illusion that I was in control of how I was being treated. The truth is, I have never been in control of others' behaviour, and many things I have taken responsibility for have not been my fault. Other people's emotions, thoughts and behaviours extend far beyond what I do and say. I remind myself of that as much as I can.

Strengthening your boundaries

Boundaries are limits or guidelines that separate your needs and responsibilities from those of others. Having clear boundaries is one of the most effective ways a person can protect their relationships, self-esteem, energy levels, time, space, money and so on. Boundaries often overlap with responsibilities. Someone who lacks boundaries might take on everyone else's problems or, on the other hand, expect others to solve all of their problems for them.

People without clear boundaries often feel guilty when saying 'no' to others. As a consequence, they may end up doing things that don't bring them meaning or enjoyment, that make them feel uncomfortable, or that they don't have the time or energy to do. Sometimes people don't have clear boundaries because they think that others' needs are more important than their own. As a result, they may use every last drop of their time, energy and skills on fulfilling others' needs, leaving little time, space, energy or money left for themselves and the things that they value. Without boundaries, a person can easily feel unfulfilled, undervalued and exhausted.

Until a few years ago, I struggled with setting boundaries because I felt so guilty whenever I put myself first. I had to 'balance the emotion' (see Chapter 7) to do something for myself regardless of how guilty it made me feel. The more I commit to my boundaries, the more deserving I feel of the time and space I make for myself. Boundaries make managing my BPD easier – not only because I have enough time and space for myself, but because I feel worthy of spending time and energy on my wellbeing. I wanted to share some examples of how clear boundaries might sound:

- I have an appointment at 6 pm, so I can't stay late. However, I can do it tomorrow when I arrive at work.
- I can stay at the party for two hours.
- Please don't use that language when my children are here.
- I'm seeing my friend this weekend, so I can't meet you. I am free next weekend, though, if that works for you?
- Please don't make comments about my body shape.
- I'm going home now as I don't want to stay at your house today.
- I can't afford to buy that.

If someone is not respecting your boundaries, it is important to evaluate your relationship with them. Everyone deserves to have their boundaries respected, just as everyone is worthy of setting them in the first place.

Managing feedback and criticism

Whilst feedback is less judgemental and more supportive than criticism, I usually find receiving both extremely difficult. A piece of feedback or an instance of criticism is always part of a much bigger picture, yet in the moment I tend to feel that it defines me. When my partner tells me that it is easier for him to talk to me after he has made coffee (rather than the minute he wakes up and is sleepy), I am flooded with shame, guilt, fear and sadness. My immediate thoughts are likely to be anxious and judgemental: Do I talk too much? Is he fed up with me? Why do I never shut up? I tend to over-personalize and over-generalize feedback or criticism ('I do not like talking to you, please never talk to me ever again'), rather than noticing the context and specifics of what is actually being expressed ('Please talk to when I am more awake'). In the time it takes to hear a few words and think a few thoughts, I can go from feeling positive about myself and my relationships to thinking that I am unlovable and fearing abandonment.

Without a doubt, managing over-personalizing and over-generalizing feedback and criticism is one of my biggest challenges. As my thoughts, emotions and urges can be so strong, using the SOS technique (as outlined in Chapter 7) helps me to pause. Reflecting on the following points helps me put feedback or criticism into perspective and soothe the pain that has been activated:

- Notice that this feedback or criticism is one in hundreds, thousands or even millions of things that this person has said to you.
- Ask yourself whether the feedback is coming from a caring place. Perhaps someone is giving feedback because they value their relationship with you and they know that you value their needs enough to adapt the way you do something. Maybe they are critiquing your work because they see your full potential and want to help you extend your skills.
- If the criticism is coming from a supportive place, see what you can learn. Use it as an opportunity to talk with others about new approaches, ways of thinking or relating to others. Remember that although this feedback hurts right now, explore whether it could actually direct you towards a more fulfilling life.

If criticism is not coming from a caring place, give yourself permission to disregard it. You don't have the time or energy to have someone rain on your parade. Do whatever you can to protect yourself from this kind of criticism in the future. Validate the understandable pain you feel using the self-validation script in Chapter 7. If memories of unsupportive criticism keep returning, notice the thoughts without judging them and let them pass (see Chapter 7).

Notice that giving feedback is a skill that not everyone has honed. Some people give feedback in a humble, graceful way, whilst others share it heavy-handedly or even arrogantly. If someone offers feedback clumsily and it has hurt you, think about whether this was due to unkind intentions or being inexperienced at offering criticism.

If someone offers feedback in a patronizing or superior manner, it may be a warning sign that they are trying to exert their power over you in an unfair way. This is unacceptable.

Criticism and feedback (even when coming from a caring place) can activate distressing thoughts of self-harm and suicide in some people with BPD. Have a look at Chapter 8, which explores self-harm and suicide, or contact emergency services if immediate help is needed.

Celebrating positives

Without a doubt, people with BPD are often exceptionally caring, thoughtful and understanding individuals. On the many occasions that I have been in crisis, my empathy and concern for others have fled the scene along with my usual etiquette and social norms. Yet, the vast majority of the time, I empathize so naturally that I barely notice I'm doing it.

Because people with this condition know that a small act of support can make a huge difference, they are often especially generous with their time, skills and emotions. When I was suicidal and staff members at the café smiled as they handed the coffee to me, it made me feel that maybe (just maybe) things could be okay. A tiny action meant so much to me in that moment of despair. As this book acknowledges, many people with BPD know stigma and discrimination intimately. As a result, it's hard to find a person with BPD who will judge someone or something before they know the full details. Those who have been misunderstood and misrepresented are unlikely to invalidate others' thoughts and feelings because they know how much that hurts.

Most, if not all, people with BPD have huge amounts of strength and determination. A lot of the time, these qualities are shown quietly or privately, which means they can go un-noticed by others. When I graduated from university in 2014, everyone generously congratulated me on my degree. However, I felt that it wasn't the academic success that needed celebrating as much as the fact that I had survived so many days and nights of feeling suicidal. Each day I had got out of bed to go to a lecture or the library after crying until the small hours the previous night took a force of will. Asking for help after being repeatedly dismissed or mocked required tenac-ity. In the last few years, therapists have praised me for my hard work when I have been able to implement new coping techniques. My response has always been to thank them, but I explain that I actually showed much more determination in the past when I didn't know the coping techniques, but nevertheless made enormous efforts just to stay alive.

I might not seem courageous, but I know it is one of my defining qualities. Bravery means staring fear in the face, acknowledging the risk, feeling terror and then doing what needs doing regardless. Each time I have told someone the truth about my BPD, bared my hurts in therapy, stood up to professionals who stigmatized me and took up space when I didn't feel worthy, I did it thanks to courage. Bravery was not giving a speech in front of hundreds of people when I won a Mind Media Award. Courage is in everyday decisions and actions. People with BPD are often courageous because no matter how frightened they are feeling, each day they do things that terrify them – speaking to someone, asking a question, looking for help. I encourage you to notice your many strengths and to acknowledge the positive qualities you bring to relationships and life in general.

The value of peer support

A few years ago, I wanted to join a peer support group so I could chat in person with others diagnosed with BPD and learn from them, but I couldn't find any. I decided to meet in person with someone I had spoken with on Twitter who, a little while later, became one of my closest and most loved friends. We can make each other feel understood in ways that other people can't because our experiences are so closely matched. As a result, we intuitively know what to say when one of us is in distress and guide each other to a calmer, more comfortable place. I have many friends with mental health problems, but I cannot relate fully to their experiences because they seem quite different to mine. I recommend seeing if peer support could bring you the same comfort it has brought me. If you meet up with someone you met online, do it safely, though. Always meet in a busy, public place and take someone with you or tell someone where you're going. Remember also to never give someone personal details such as your address until you can safely trust them.

Are you being respected?

People frequently contact me asking for advice about their relationships. Often they ask how they can feel calmer and happier in a relationship whilst describing being treated disrespectfully or abusively. I always feel sad to think of people trying to feel calmer and happier in a relationship that is full of cruelty or maltreatment. I don't want anyone to work on feeling calmer, only to get no joy (and blame themselves) because their efforts are being undermined by someone else. Regardless of the effort a person puts into a relationship, if it is disrespectful or abusive, it's like trying to stay dry in a shipwreck. It's pointless – and I speak from personal experience.

It is more than possible to strengthen relationships, make them calmer and happier, but only when it's a relationship built on mutual respect, kindness and support. Please only put effort into relationships where your efforts will be supported and not spoilt. I know how hard it can be to recognize abusive relationships given the complicated mixture of feelings and circumstances often involved.

Is it a healthy relationship?

If you answer 'yes' to the following questions, this is a good indicator that the relationship has healthy foundations. This relationship is likely to provide opportunities for feeling calmer and happier, rather than deepening your distress or generating further emotional pain.

Does this person:

- Help me live according to my values?
- Give me a sense of enjoyment or wellbeing?
- Treat my needs and wishes as important?
- Respect my choices in terms of what I do, who I spend time with, my appearance, finances and how I live my life?
- Only do sexual or physical things when I consent and feel comfortable?
- Take me seriously when I speak up about a problem in the relationship?
- Have a respectful and compassionate stance towards my mental health problems?

When I am around this person, do I feel:

- Safe?
- Free to make my own choices?
- Valued?
- Respected?
- That my needs and wishes are as important as theirs?

Abusive relationships

Abuse in relationships can be subtle and difficult to recognize. People who are abusive to others often play 'mind games' to make others think their behaviour is acceptable. If you answer 'yes' to the following questions, this relationship is indicating signs of abuse. I urge you to seek support using the 'Resources' at the end of this book or by speaking to someone you trust.

Does this person:

- Treat my needs and wishes as unimportant?
- Control what I do, who I spend time with, my appearance, finances or life choices?
- Insult, name call, mock or put me down?
- Tell me that I am imagining problems or being overly sensitive when I speak up about how I am being treated?
- Blame me for things that are not my fault or that are out of my control?
- Physically hurt me or threaten to hurt me (or people I love)?
- Do sexual things or things with my body without my consent and when I am not comfortable?
- Intrude on my privacy?
- Treat me in ways that I wouldn't want my friends or family to know about?
- Mock, bully or blame me for having mental health problems?
- Tell me that I deserve to feel upset, hurt myself or die?

When I am around this person, do I feel:

- Scared?
- Controlled?

- Exploited?
- Like I can't do anything right?
- That my needs and wishes do not matter or are less important than theirs?
- More like an object than a person with feelings?

There are 'Resources' at the end of this book for anyone who is in (or thinks they might be in) an abusive relationship. It is always worth seeking some objective advice about the relationship or support and guidance on possibly leaving, including making a safe exit plan.

BPD and romantic relationships

After being told in my early twenties that I was "too difficult", "too messed up" and "too emotional" to love, it brings me huge joy to be in a relationship with someone who loves my personality and feels good in my company. I have been in this happy, calm relationship for a few years, and now we even have a puppy together! Quite a lot of my blog readers have expressed interest in what makes my relationship work so well, so I thought I would share my thoughts here, in case they might be useful. Whilst friendships and romantic relationships share many overlapping features, the intensity and physicality of romantic relationships usually sets the two apart. As you may know, the intensity of a romantic relationship gives rise to ideal conditions for the activation of powerful and painful emotions. However, healthy romantic relationships can open up new and fruitful ways of relating to others, sharing emotions and experiencing the world.

Compatibility

My partner and I have very similar values and outlooks, which means that we both want the same kinds of things in life. We have a number of interests in common that we can enjoy together and some that we don't share, which we can do without each other. Our personalities complement each other well because we have some traits in common (we are both creative, playful and hardworking) and others that balance one another (my partner is cool-headed and logical, whereas I am excitable and restless). In a romantic relationship more than a friendship, I think compatibility lies in the balance of similarities and differences between the partners. Too similar and there may be an overabundance of one trait in the relationship; too different and finding compromises may prove difficult.

Learning together

My partner and I approach my BPD as something we learn about together. I tell him my thoughts about something, he responds with his viewpoint, and we keep going until we reach a shared understanding. I work on the principle that no human can ever *fully* understand another, and if someone is trying to understand, then that's absolutely enough! I accept that my partner will never know how I feel when I am sobbing on the floor wanting to hurt myself. Yet, he is able to give me so much in those moments by staying calm, sharing kind words, validating my feelings, hugging me and reminding me to do DBT skills. That is absolutely wonderful, entirely enough, and I tell him so.

Learning to manage BPD effectively in the context of

romantic relationships is most definitely a process of trial and error. Both partners will come up with ideas that seem like they will be effective, but when applied in the moment turn out to be fruitless. That's okay. Explore whether the idea will work under different circumstances or whether an entirely new approach is needed.

Openness and honesty

My partner and I try not to assume that we know what the other is thinking or feeling without telling them. We find that most misunderstandings can be solved quickly if both partners explain their thought processes. It usually turns out that one partner assumed that the other knew what they were thinking when they didn't! Our relationship only runs as smoothly as it does because my partner is as honest about his needs and feeling as I am about mine. If I do something that annoys him or makes him sad, he will tell me, even though he knows that I may cry or have a panic attack afterwards. We know that in order to protect the integrity of our relationship, he needs to tell me how he feels regardless of whether a meltdown follows.

I appreciate the courage he shows every time he is open with me about something that might activate painful emotions in me. Furthermore, when he is honest with me about something that might upset me, he gives me the opportunity to learn that a moment of insensitivity doesn't make me unlovable. I think that over the next couple of years I will reach a place where I don't panic when I do something less than ideal in our relationship.

Humour

Around a year or so into our relationship, my partner and I started using humour as a way of defusing my anxiety, especially my fear of abandonment. He is the kind of person who jokes all the time, so it was only natural for us to joke about this too. Of course, humour like this is not for everyone, but my partner and I find it helpful.

Communicating boundaries gently

My partner knows that I tend to experience boundaries as cold and rejecting, even though I know they exist to support the relationship and the needs of both people involved. However, it helps me immensely that my partner communicates his boundaries with gentleness. He validates my emotions before he asserts his limits: "I know you are anxious today and you want to talk to me now, but I am in the middle of something. Let's talk about it after work when I can concentrate fully." This gentle assertiveness means the boundaries feel less threatening and more supportive – more like garden fences than concrete walls laced with barbed wire.

CHAPTER 10

Finding Identity and Meaning

I know that some people with BPD struggle with identifying their values and finding a direction in life that feels meaningful. In spite of having difficulties with a shifting self-image (as described in Chapter 2), I have never struggled with knowing who I am, what my values are and how I want to live my life. Furthermore, my multiple privileges of being white, middle-class, cis-gender and able-bodied have always enabled me to take up space, express my identity and live according to my values without fearing for my safety or compromising my wellbeing.

As a result of conversations with others, I realize life can be tiring and confusing without a sense of identity or an understanding of what makes life feel fulfilling. This final chapter shares a few techniques drawn from various therapies that I hope can support anyone who is trying to understand their values better or figure out their next steps. These techniques also work just as well for individuals who, like me, want to make sure their actions are guided by their values rather than flurries of emotion.

Values-guided action

I was introduced to Dr Russ Harris' concept of 'values-guided action' when I had a few sessions of acceptance and commitment therapy (ACT). This concept has helped me take control of days and weeks when I am feeling so upset that I don't want to do anything except lie in bed and cry. Values-guided action means doing things that are led by your values, even when uncomfortable thoughts or painful emotions arise (Harris 2019). The idea is that values-guided action can help a person lead a more meaningful life. Let me explain a little.

In ACT, values are likened to a compass that gives directions for travel in life (Harris 2019, p.11). However, as ACT therapist Russ Harris points out, 'we won't have much of a journey if we simply stare at the compass; our journey only happens when we move [...] in our chosen direction' (Harris 2019, p.11). I will share an example of values-guided action from my life. One of my values is putting time and energy into friendships. Most weekends, my friend and I talk on the phone for around an hour to catch up on each other's lives. My values are driving my actions, or, to use the metaphor, my compass is showing the way and I am moving in that direction. Recently, though, I have been feeling fear of abandonment, and last week I felt so anxious that I wanted to cancel our phone call. In spite of my fears, I reminded myself of my value of friendship, the love and connection I feel, and picked up the phone. My actions were driven by my values rather than my upsetting thoughts.

Of course, doing things that are guided by our values rather than our state of mind is easier said than done. As someone easily swept away by intense emotions, I have needed to master DBT-based coping techniques to get me to a place where my actions are guided by values rather than moods. Whilst I don't have space in this book to explore values-guided action in depth, I hope that the next few paragraphs can provide a useful taster or inspire you to learn more from books and websites.

Identifying your values

Some people (like me) know their values almost instinctively. For others, identifying their values takes longer. One of the most common techniques for identifying values that I have seen in self-help books involves looking at a long list of words, such as kindness, knowledge, equality, family and determination, and circling the ones that resonate most.

If this typical technique for identifying values doesn't bring any clarity, I suggest making a list of people you admire. These could be people you know, individuals in the public eye or even fictional characters. Next to their names, write down what it is you like about them. What is it about them that you admire? What appeals to you about the way they think, act, express themselves or relate to others? Make some notes and see if any common themes emerge.

. Most people learn throughout childhood, through their family, schooling and environment as a whole, that certain values hold more importance than others. As a child, my family, school and rural surroundings taught me to value kindness, resourcefulness, respect for others and nature. I still hold these same values all those years later, as well as having taken on new values of self-expression, tenacity and speaking up for what I believe in.

Because values tend to be embedded during childhood, it can be hard to feel 'allowed' to change your values or take on new ones. Be compassionate with yourself because, unless your values damage others, there is no right or wrong when it comes to this. If this exercise is painful, or if your mind feels blank, take a break and gently return to it as many times as you need.

Aligning actions with values

Whenever I want to align my actions with my values, first, I need to accept my thoughts and feelings. Often, my thoughts and emotions are at odds with values-driven action. For example, one of my values is to preserve some time for myself so I can get the rest I need to stay healthy. Actions in line with this value include finishing work on time, only saying 'yes' to things I can manage and giving myself permission to chill in front of the TV when I'm tired. However, sometimes I think 'I don't deserve to rest', 'I should work for another hour' or feel anxious and guilty when I rest.

When I find myself resisting acting on my values, it is helpful to notice my thoughts without judging them. I tell myself 'Thank you thoughts and feelings, but I am going to rest because resting is one of my values'. As you can imagine, this will not make the uncomfortable thoughts and feelings magically disappear, although it may help lessen their power over you. Acknowledging any thoughts or feelings about resisting values-driven action but going ahead nonetheless can be uncomfortable and even scary. However, the reward for taking such a leap of faith is doing more things that bring meaning and fulfilment to your life. This aspect of ACT definitely taught me that I can take part in meaningful activities, in spite of having thoughts and emotions that tell me otherwise.

Radical acceptance

There are some aspects of life that I can control and others that – no matter how hard I try – I cannot. Like many people, I have spent periods of my life wishing I could go back in time and change the course of events or travel into the future to secure a desired outcome. Longing for things to be different when they simply cannot be any other way is usually deeply painful. Spending time and energy desperately trying to change something that is outside of your control is exhausting, frustrating and disheartening.

If you're anything like me, you will know the anguish of desperately wanting someone to say a certain thing or behave in a specific way towards you. There have been times when I have been so desperate for a connection with someone that I would have done almost anything to get someone to reply to my texts, return my phone calls or give me the tiniest shred of affection. As painful as it is to accept this, I know I cannot make others love me or want to connect with me.

The DBT skill 'radical acceptance' helps me manage situations that I do not want to endure but am not able to change (Linehan 2015). It is also effective when I want to know something, but there is no way of knowing. Radical acceptance involves acknowledging when a situation or an outcome is outside of my control, and accepting that there is nothing I can do to change the state of affairs. To radically accept a situation is to let go of all attempts to solve problems, influence outcomes or change how others feel. The decision to radically accept a situation is not a one-off resolution that happens easily or quickly. Radical acceptance involves repeatedly acknowledging and accepting when you do not have influence over something. Whenever I catch myself longing for things to be different or trying to change something that I cannot alter, I acknowledge what is going on, how painful that is, and then remind myself that I cannot change it. Radical acceptance doesn't take away the pain caused by difficult situations, but it frees up time and energy to focus on the things that are in my control.

As someone who feels safest when I am in control, radical acceptance usually involves a frightening leap of faith. However, I have found that the scarier the leap, the bigger the sense of peace that follows. As I write this chapter, I am going through an extremely difficult situation that is outside of my control. Every couple of hours, and as strong urges to alter this situation arise, I am reminding myself to radically accept what is happening. Radical acceptance is hard, but not using it is harder.

The inner child

In one of my final group sessions of DBT, one of the therapists explained something that resonated with me. With heartfelt conviction, this therapist told the group that when we experience emotional distress, we need the same things we needed as small children: to be soothed, comforted and understood.

She talked about the idea of the 'inner child' (several forms of which can be found in Jungian therapy, transactional analysis and other types of psychotherapy), and explained that when we are distressed, our 'inner child' may be feeling frightened or sad. Talk to yourself in the same way you would speak to a child in your care who is upset, she urged. Would you shout at a crying child and tell them the same cruel things you say to yourself? Talk to yourself kindly and show yourself care, she said.

Even though this therapist was encouraging me to try something completely alien to me, the earnestness and compassion with which she expressed her belief were so compelling that I couldn't resist trying it out. There are moments when, lying on my bed drowning in shame or sadness, I talk gently to myself as if I were soothing a child. As I often feel as vulnerable and terrified as an infant during times of distress, it makes sense that relating to myself in this way can bring calm. Looking after others comes naturally to me. Looking after myself is something I have had to learn, as if it were a new language. I still don't always get it right and I make mistakes.

So long as I keep practising, I know that one day I will be fluent in self-compassion. I hope you can look inside yourself when you're feeling distressed and see if you have a scared or sad inner child. See what this child needs and how you can provide for this, even if it feels like reaching into the dark for something you cannot see.

The possibility of embracing sensitivity?

My BPD is the result of my innate emotional sensitivity in combination with difficult experiences during my childhood and adolescence. With only one of these aspects, but not the other, I wouldn't have BPD. If I had a magic wand, would I erase my emotional sensitivity? Absolutely not.

Being sensitive to my own and others' emotions brings my life a richness and a luminosity that it would lack if my emotions were more muted. Being a highly emotional person is like painting with highly pigmented colours – every brushstroke is strong, every emotion is vivid. Without my emotional sensitivity I don't think I would love books, art, poetry or nature in the same way. If my emotions were dampened down, perhaps I wouldn't be in an empathetic, people-centred career. It is thanks to my emotional nature that I feel deeply, love fiercely and give generously.

Sometimes it feels like this world wants to crush emotional sensitivity, especially in boys and men. However, emotional sensitivity is a luminous quality that ought not to be dimmed. It is a glowing characteristic in a person; it is courageous, giving and brings the possibility of connection. Emotionally sensitive people illuminate avenues for care, closeness and healing that others without the same emotional intensity often do not. Each time I am made vulnerable by my emotions, it opens up opportunities to connect with others, to learn and feel things I might never otherwise have felt. Sometimes this hurts, and sometimes this brings joy. I have come to accept both of those things and to see them as gifts.

Whilst I would not erase my emotional sensitivity if I were given the chance, do I wish I had never developed BPD as a result of difficult life experiences? That's a more difficult question to answer. In the last decade, there have been times when I would have given anything to remove the pain

I felt: my suicidal thoughts have borne witness to that agony. However, my BPD has revealed my resourcefulness and my resilience. In many ways, I am proud to have this condition because it indicates my strength. It also reveals that without vulnerability, there is no such thing as strength.

In the same breath, though, I know that not everyone with this diagnosis has had the same chances at feeling better as me. I have been lucky and I am indebted to my family and friends for their care. I am infinitely sad for all those people who had this agonizing condition and are no longer with us. In order to prevent more brilliant people losing their lives to this condition, much more needs to be done so that every individual gets the care and support they need, and especially those from groups marginalized by society.

I would never tell anyone to love their emotional sensitivity or be grateful for the difficulties they have been through. For many people, it doesn't feel at all right to embrace aspects of themselves or things that have happened that are associated with immense pain. For me, though, I find it helpful to not only respect, but also to celebrate my emotional sensitivity. After all, if I weren't an emotionally sensitive person, I wouldn't be the person I am, be so close to the people I love or do the things that mean so much to me. Not only that, but part of me is proud of my survival as someone with BPD. In a society that too often fears, devalues or writes off people with this condition, my life has often felt heavy and complicated. It still feels that way sometimes. I have to cry and breathe and take refuge until the feeling passes.

Although at times my shame has almost smothered me, I have been able to see beyond it. I resolve to claim my identity on my own terms, and this book is part of that process. I am Rosie. I have BPD. I am not an attention seeker, manipulative, dangerous, hopeless, unlovable, 'broken', 'difficult to reach' or 'unwilling to engage'. I am caring, creative, courageous, determined, and full of life and love.

I hope this book has helped you see all of the wonderful things you are, so you can worry less about all the things you are not. You are not a stereotype. You are not undeserving of care. You are not unworthy of love. You are a person who feels a lot and has been through so much. You are lovable. You are worthy. If you can't cling onto a thread of hope right now, you can find me right here – holding on to it until you can.

References

Aguirre, B. and Galen, G. (2013) *Mindfulness for Borderline Personality Disorder: Relieve Your Suffering Using the Core Skill of Dialectical Behavior Therapy*. Oakland, CA: New Harbinger.

APA (American Psychiatric Association) (2013) *Diagnostic and Statistical Manual of Mental Disorders* (DSM-5) (5th edn). Washington, DC: APA.

Aviram, R., Brodsky, B. and Stanley, B. (2006) 'Borderline personality disorder, stigma, and treatment implications.' *Harvard Review of Psychiatry 14*, 5, 249–256.

Bachmann, C. and Gooch, B. (2018) *LGBT in Britain – Health*. Stonewall. Available at: www.stonewall.org.uk/lgbt-britain-health

Baker, B. (2010) *Diary Drawings: Mental Illness and Me*. London: Profile Books.

Bateman, A. and Fonagy, P. (2010) 'Mentalization based treatment for borderline personality disorder.' *World Psychiatry 9*, 1, 11–15.

Bhui, K., Nazroo, J., Francis, J., Halvorsrud, K., Rhodes, J. and the Synergi Collaborative Centre (2018) 'The impact of racism on mental health.' Available at: https://synergicollaborativecentre.co.uk/wp-content/uploads/2017/11/The-impact-of-racism-on-mental-health-briefing-paper-1.pdf

Biskin, R.S. (2015) 'The lifetime course of borderline personality disorder.' *Canadian Journal of Psychiatry 60*, 7, 303–308.

Biskin, R.S. and Paris, J. (2013) 'Comorbidities in borderline personality disorder.' *Psychiatric Times Online*, 10 January. Available at: www.psychiatrictimes.com/view/comorbidities-borderline-personality-disorder

Bui, E., Rodgers, R., Chabrol, H., Birmes, P. and Schmitt, L. (2011) 'Is Anakin Skywalker suffering from borderline personality disorder?' *Psychiatry Research 185*, 1–2, 299.

Carey, B. (2011) 'Expert on mental illness reveals her own fight.' *The New York Times*, 23 June. Available at: www.nytimes.com/2011/06/23/health/23lives.html

Carlson, E.B., Palmieri, P.A., Field, N.P., Dalenberg, C.J., Macia, K.S. and Spain, D.A. (2016) 'Contributions of risk and protective factors to prediction of psychological symptoms after traumatic experiences.' *Comprehensive Psychiatry 69*, 106–115.

Carroll, S. (2019) 'Surviving manipulative people.' Available at: https://scottcarrollmd.com/surviving-manipulative-people/

Carollo, K. (2011) 'NFL star Brandon Marshall has borderline personality disorder.' ABC News, 1 August. Available at: https://abcnews.go.com/Health/miami-dolphins-wide-receiver-brandon-marshall-reveals-borderline/story?id=14204660

Choi-Kain, L.W., Finch, E.F., Masland, S.R., Jenkins, J.A. and Unruh, B.T. (2017) 'What works in the treatment of borderline personality disorder.' *Current Behavioral Neuroscience Reports 4*, 1, 21–30.

Cipriano, A., Cella, S. and Cotrufo, P. (2017) 'Nonsuicidal self-injury: A systematic review.' *Frontiers in Psychology 8*, 1946. Available at: www.frontiersin.org/articles/10.3389/fpsyg.2017.01946/full

Clearview Women's Center (no date) 'Tips for interacting with a coworker with BPD.' Available at: www.borderlinepersonalitytreatment.com/coworker-with-borderline-personality-disorder.html

Corstens, D., Longden, E., McCarthy-Jones, S., Waddingham, R. and Thomas, N. (2014) 'Emerging perspectives from the Hearing Voices Movement: Implications for research and practice.' *Schizophrenia Bulletin 40*, 4, S285–S294.

Drescher, J., North, C. and Suris, A. (2015) 'Out of DSM: Depathologizing homosexuality.' *Behavioral Sciences 5*, 4, 565–575.

Eddy, B. (2018) *5 Types of People Who Can Ruin Your Life: Identifying and Dealing with Narcissists, Sociopaths, and Other High-Conflict Personalities*. New York: Tarcher Perigree.

Edmondson, J., Brennan, C. and House, A. (2016) 'Non-suicidal reasons for self-harm: A systematic review of self-reported account.' *Journal of Affective Disorder 191*, 109–117.

Elam, P. (2016) 'Shutting down your borderline ex: Chainsaw style.' YouTube. Available at: www.youtube.com/watch?v=4cfzC7aPztA

Forsyth, A. (2007) 'The effects of diagnosis and non-compliance attributions on therapeutic alliance processes in adult acute psychiatric settings.' *Journal of Psychiatric Mental Health Nursing 14*, 1, 33–40.

Frankl, F. (2019) 'Media portrayal of mental illness does more harm than good.' *The Statesman*, 6 October. Available at: www.sbstatesman. com/2019/10/06/media-portrayal-of-mental-illness-does-more-harm-than-good

French, L., Moran, P., Wiles, N., Kessler, D. and Turner, K.M. (2019) 'GPs' views and experiences of managing patients with personality disorder: a qualitative interview study.' *BMJ Open 9*, 2. Available at: https:// doi.org/10.1136/bmjopen-2018-026616

Fruzzetti, A.E. (2017) 'Why borderline personality disorder is misdiagnosed.' National Alliance on Mental Illness Blog, 3 October. Available at: www.nami.org/Blogs/NAMI-Blog/October-2017/Why-Borderline-Personality-Disorder-is-Misdiagnose

Gallop, R., Lancee, W.J. and Garfinkel, P. (1989) 'How nursing staff respond to the label "borderline personality disorder".' *Hospital & Community Psychiatry 40*, 8, 815–819.

Goffman, E. (1963) *Stigma: Notes on the Management of Spoiled Identity*. New York: Simon & Schuster.

Griffiths, M.D. (2013) 'Fiddler of the truth.' *Psychology Today*, 11 October. Available at: www.psychologytoday.com/gb/blog/in-excess/201310/ fiddler-the-truth

Gunderson, J.G. (1996) 'The borderline patient's intolerance of aloneness: insecure attachments and therapist availability.' *American Journal of Psychiatry 153*, 6, 752–758.

Gunderson, J.G. (2009) 'Borderline personality disorder: Ontogeny of a diagnosis.' *American Journal of Psychiatry 166*, 5, 530–539.

Harris, R. (2019) *ACT Made Simple: An Easy-to-Read Primer on Acceptance and Commitment Therapy* (Second edition). Oakland, CA: New Harbinger.

Harvard Health Publishing (2019) 'Borderline Personality Disorder.' Harvard Health Publishing, Harvard Medical School. Available at: https://www. health.harvard.edu/a_to_z/borderline-personality-disorder-a-to-z.

Hattenstone, S. (2020) 'BPD and me: How comedian Joe Tracini saved his own life – and gave hope to others.' *The Guardian*: G2, 17 August. Available at: www.theguardian.com/society/2020/aug/17/bpd-and-me-how-comedian-joe-tracini-saved-his-own-life-and-gave-hope-to-others

Klonsky, D. (2009) 'The functions of self-injury in young adults who cut themselves: Clarifying the evidence for affect regulation.' *Psychiatry Research 166*, 2, 3 260–268.

Koekkoek, B., van Meijel, B. and Hutschemaekers, G. (2006) '"Difficult patients" in mental health care: A review.' *Psychiatric Services 57*, 6, 795–802.

Kreisman, J. and Straus, H. (1991) *I Hate You – Don't Leave Me: Understanding Borderline Personality Disorder*. New York: Avon Books. [Original work published in 1989 in Los Angeles by The Body Press.]

Kreisman, J. and Straus, H. (2004) *Sometimes I Act Crazy: Living with Borderline Personality Disorder*. San Francisco, CA: Jossey-Bass.

Lancer, D. (2019) 'The drama of loving a borderline.' *Psychology Today*, 5 September. Available at: www.psychologytoday.com/gb/blog/toxic-relationships/201909/the-drama-loving-borderline

Linehan, M.M. (1993) *Cognitive-Behavioral Treatment of Borderline Personality Disorder*. New York: Guilford Press.

Linehan, M.M. (2015) *DBT Skills Training Handouts and Worksheets* (Second edition). New York: Guilford Press.

Link, B.G. and Phelan, J. (2014) 'Stigma power.' *Social Science & Medicine 103*, 24–32.

Maguire, E.A., Gadian, D.G., Johnsrude, I.S., Good, C.D. *et al.* (2000) 'Navigation-related structural change in the hippocampi of taxi drivers.' *PNAS: Proceedings of the National Academy of Sciences of the United States of America 97*, 8, 4398–4403.

McNeil, J., Bailey, L., Ellis, S., Morton, J. and Regan, M. (2012) *Trans Mental Health Study 2012*. Edinburgh: Scottish Transgender Alliance. Available at: www.scottishtrans.org/wp-content/uploads/2013/03/trans_mh_study.pdf

Mental Health Foundation (2015) 'Stigma and discrimination.' Available at: www.mentalhealth.org.uk/a-to-z/s/stigma-and-discrimination

Mental Welfare Commission for Scotland (2018) 'Visit and Monitoring Report, Living with Borderline Personality Disorder.' Available at: https://www.mwcscot.org.uk/sites/default/files/2019-06/nov2018bpd_report_final.pdf

Meyer-Lindenberg, A. (2009) 'The roots of problem personalities.' *Scientific American Mind*, April. Available at: www.scientificamerican.com/article/perturbed-personalities/

Mind (2021) 'Complex post-traumatic stress disorder (complex PTSD).' Available at: www.mind.org.uk/information-support/types-of-mental-health-problems/post-traumatic-stress-disorder-ptsd-and-complex-ptsd/complex-ptsd/

Moynihan, R. (2011) 'A new deal on disease definition.' *British Medical Journal 324*, 7342, 1054–1056.

Mulay, A.L., Waugh, M.H., Parks Fillauer, J., Bender, D.S. *et al.* (2019) 'Borderline personality disorder diagnosis in a new key.' *Borderline Personality Disorder and Emotional Dysregulation 6*, 1. Available at: https://bpded.biomedcentral.com/articles/10.1186/s40479-019-0116-1

NICE (National Institute for Health and Care Excellence) (2009) *Borderline Personality Disorder: Recognition and Management.* London: Department of Health.

NIMH (National Institute for Mental Health in England) (2003) *Personality Disorder: No Longer a Diagnosis of Exclusion.* London: Department of Health.

Nowinski, J. (2014) *Hard to Love: Understanding and Overcoming Male Borderline Personality Disorder.* Las Vegas, NV: Central Recovery Press.

Porter, C., Palmier-Claus, J., Branitsky, A., Mansell, W., Warwick, H. and Varese, F. (2020) 'Childhood adversity and borderline personality disorder: A meta-analysis.' *Acta Psychiatrica Scandinavica 141*, 1, 6–20.

Pungong, C. (2017) 'On the realities of being a black woman with borderline personality disorder.' *Do What You Want Zine*, 114–119.

Randy, K. and Mason, P. (1998) *Stop Walking on Eggshells: Taking Your Life Back When Someone You Care About Has Borderline Personality Disorder.* New York: MJF Books.

Rethink Mental Illness (no date) 'Borderline personality disorder.' Available at: www.rethink.org/advice-and-information/about-mental-illness/learn-more-about-conditions/borderline-personality-disorder/

RITB (Recovery in the Bin) (2019) 'RITP position statement on borderline personality disorder.' 3 April. Available at: https://recoveryinthebin.org/2019/04/03/ritb-position-statement-on-borderline-personality-disorder

Rosenberg, R. (2014) 'Pt 2. The impossible connection: Loving someone w/ borderline personality disorder: See warning.' YouTube. Available at: www.youtube.com/watch?v=3bfKLJ5YGyQYouTube

Royal College of Psychiatry (2020) 'Services for people diagnosable with personality disorder: Position statement.' London: Royal College of Psychiatry.

Ruggero, C., Zimmerman, M., Chelminski, I. and Young, D. (2010) 'Borderline personality disorder and the misdiagnosis of bipolar disorder.' *Journal of Psychiatric Research 44*, 6, 405–408.

SAMHSA (Substance Abuse and Mental Health Services Administration) Trauma and Justice Strategic Initiative (2014) 'Concept of trauma and guidance for a trauma-informed approach.' US Department of Health and Human Services. Rockville, MD: Substance Abuse and Mental Health Services, Administration Office of Policy, Planning and Innovation. Available at: https://ncsacw.samhsa.gov/userfiles/files/SAMHSA_Trauma.pdf

Sandman, C.A. and Kemp, A.S. (2011) 'Opioid antagonists may reverse endogenous opiate "dependence" in the treatment of self-injurious behavior.' *Pharmaceuticals 4*, 2, 366–381.

Sansone, R. and Sansone, L. (2011) 'Gender patterns in borderline personality disorder.' *Innovations in Clinical Neuroscience 8*, 5, 16–20.

Stevenson, R.L. (2002) *The Strange Case of Dr Jekyll and Mr Hyde and Other Tales of Terror*. R. Mighall (ed.). London: Penguin Books Ltd. [Original work published 1886.]

Stone, M.H. (2005) 'Borderline Personality Disorder: History of the Concept.' In M.C. Zanarini (ed.) *Borderline Personality Disorder* (pp.1–18). Abingdon: Taylor & Francis.

Surviving BPD Relationship Break Up (2020) 'Borderlines will cause devastation to your sanity and self-esteem.' YouTube. Available at: www.youtube.com/watch?v=S_bVHgDVitA

The Guardian (2017) 'Personality disorders at work: How to spot them and what you can do.' [Since removed.]

Thorp, N. (2020) 'Having borderline personality disorder can be exhausting but good friends don't let you feel a burden.' *Metro*, 28 February. Available at: https://metro.co.uk/2020/02/28/borderline-personality-disorder-strain-closest-friendships-12318882/

Warrender, D. (2015) 'Staff nurse perceptions of the impact of mentalization-based therapy skills training when working with borderline personality disorder in acute mental health: A qualitative study.' *Psychiatric and Mental Health Nursing 22*, 8, 623–633.

Watts, J. (2016) 'Borderline personality disorder – A diagnosis of invalidation.' Huffington Post Blog, 26 September. Available at: www.huffingtonpost.co.uk/dr-jay-watts/borderline-personality-di_b_12167212.html

Watts, J. (2018) 'How can we expect borderline personality disorder patients to trust mental health services when the staff don't trust them?' *The Independent*, 21 July. Available at: www.independent.co.uk/voices/borderline-personality-disorder-mental-health-depression-anxiety-stress-psychiatry-a8456301.html

Williams, A.J., Arcelus, J., Townsend, E. and Michail, M. (2019) 'Examining risk factors for self-harm and suicide in LGBTQ+ young people: A systematic review protocol.' *BMJ Open* 9.

Woollaston, K. and Hixenbaugh, P. (2008) '"Destructive whirlwind": Nurses' perceptions of patients diagnosed with borderline personality disorder.' *Journal of Psychiatric and Mental Health Nursing* 15, 9, 703–709.

Zanarini, M.C., Frankenburg, F.R., Bradford Reich, D., Silk, K.R., Hudson, J.I. and McSweeney, L.B. (2007) 'The subsyndromal phenomenology of borderline personality disorder: A 10-year follow-up study.' *The American Journal of Psychiatry* 164, 929–935.

Support and Resources

Books

Aguirre, B. and Galen, G. (2013) *Mindfulness for Borderline Personality Disorder: Relieve Your Suffering Using the Core Skill of Dialectical Behavior Therapy.* Oakland, CA: New Harbinger.

Linehan, M.M. (2015) *DBT Skills Training Handouts and Worksheets* (Second edition). New York: Guilford Press.

Blogs, vlogs and websites

Healing From BPD: www.youtube.com/user/HealingFromBPD

My Illustrated Mind: www.myillustratedmind.com

Talking About BPD (my website): www.talkingaboutbpd.co.uk

Support organizations and helplines
UK

Mind: www.mind.org.uk

Refuge: 0808 2000 247, www.nationaldahelpline.org.uk

Rethink Mental Illness: www.rethink.org

Samaritans: 116 123, www.samaritans.org

Shout: Text 85258, www.giveusashout.org

Switchboard: 0300 330 0630, https://switchboard.lgbt

USA and Canada

Crisis Services Canada: 1 833 456 4566

Crisis Text Line (USA and Canada): Text: 741741, www.crisis-textline.org

National Domestic Violence Hotline (USA): 1 800 799 7233, www.ndvh.org

National Educational Alliance for Borderline Personality Disorder (NEABPD) (USA): www.borderlinepersonalitydisorder.org

National Suicide Prevention Lifeline (USA): 1 800 273 8255, www.suicidepreventionlifeline.org

Sheltersafe.ca (Canada): www.sheltersafe.ca

Trans Lifeline (USA and Canada): 877 565 8860 (USA); 877 330 6366 (Canada), https://translifeline.org

Australia and New Zealand

Lifeline (Australia): 13 11 14, www.lifeline.org.au

Lifeline (New Zealand): 0800 543 354, www.lifeline.org.nz

OUTline (New Zealand): 0800 688 5463, https://outline.org.nz

QLife (Australia): 1800 184 527, https://qlife.org.au

1800 Respect (Australia): 1800 737 732, www.1800respect.org.
au

Finding a therapist
UK

British Association for Counselling and Psychotherapy (BACP)
(UK): www.bacp.co.uk

The Black, African and Asian Therapy Network (BAATN)
(UK): www.baatn.org.uk

Pink Therapy (UK): www.pinktherapy.com

UK Council for Psychotherapy (UKCP) (UK): www.psychother-
apy.org.uk

USA and Canada

Canadian Mental Health Association (CMHA) (Canada):
https://cmha.ca/find-your-cmha

Mental Health America (MHA) Affiliate Resource Center
(USA): https://arc.mhanational.org/find-an-affiliate

Australia and New Zealand

Australia Counselling (Australia): www.australiacounselling.
com.au/find-a-therapist

Healthline (New Zealand): 0800 611 116

Acknowledgements

I would like to start by thanking my editor Jane Evans at Jessica Kingsley Publishers for recognizing the need for more supportive and non-stigmatizing books about borderline personality disorder, especially those written by people with lived experience. Thank you, Jane, my production editor Claire Robinson, and all on the editing, production, marketing and design teams who have worked together to make this book happen.

Thank you to Kimberley Wilson, author of *How to Build a Healthy Brain*, for writing such a strong Foreword. As a leader in the mental health field, I am grateful for the time and skills you have generously shared to strengthen this book. Thank you to Michelle Radcliffe, Senior Lecturer in Mental Health Nursing at Kingston University, for reviewing the manuscript. Your expertise in supporting people with a diagnosis of personality disorder meant that your feedback was invaluable and highly reassuring. Thank you also to the other mental health professionals who too offered valuable contributions to the manuscript during the review phase.

When I started my blog and social media, Talking About

BPD, in 2014 I never dreamed it would resonate so deeply with so many people. It is overwhelming to think about how many of you feel seen and validated by my writing and videos, and what's more, reciprocate by giving so much of yourselves to me in return. I want to thank every individual who has commented or tweeted me with words of connection and encouragement; your cheerleading helped me navigate agonizing shame and muster more courage than I ever knew I had. Without all of your support, I would never have experienced the solace, fulfilment, connections and opportunities that Talking About BPD has brought to my life. This book only exists because of you. I hope that reading this book brings you as much comfort, validation and self-affirmation as writing it gave me.

Thank you to the numerous individuals and organizations who have offered me a platform to talk about BPD with their audiences. Particular thanks go to Maxine Ali who wrote an article for *Happiful Magazine* in which I featured, the BBC Stories team who gave me a chance to share the positives of social media, Kimberley Wilson for inviting me onto her *Stronger Minds* podcast, the *Mentally Yours* podcast and the *Mental Health Monday* team at Radio City Talk. I would also like to thank all at Mind Media Awards for bestowing me with the 'Digital Champion' award in 2019 and for nominating me in the same category in 2017. Thank you to Michelle Radcliffe, Maxine Cromar-Hayes and all other lecturers who share Talking About BPD with student mental health nurses as part of their education on borderline personality disorder.

Infinite thanks are reserved for my teachers Miss Millhouse and Mrs Kirkham whose care and encouragement during my late teenage years still resonate in my life today. Miss Millhouse, thank you for understanding that books and writing were my lifeblood and consequently nurturing the writer in me. Mrs Kirkham, it was not just your love of language learning that meant so much to me, but the care you freely gave. Innumerable thanks to Dr Leo Mellor, Director of Studies throughout my English degree. You taught me how to critique a narrative and construct an argument, enabling me to interrogate the myths about borderline personality disorder and giving me the confidence to write a book. More than that though, when I had my initial, and terrifying, mental breakdown in my first term at university, you supported me – and didn't stop until the degree certificate was in my hand. Although not everyone saw it that way, you knew that I was invested and capable irrespective of my mental health crises. Given that one third of people who do not complete their degree do so because of mental health problems, your attitude meant a lot to me (and still does). Thank you to Dr Paola Filippucci for whole-heartedly caring for me during that frightening and confusing time. Every university student with mental health problems needs a tutor as empathetic as you.

Although I may not have met you, I want to thank the writers, artists, bloggers, zine makers and other creative individuals whose openness about their own mental health problems has emboldened me to speak up about mine. A special thank you to Jonny Benjamin MBE and Jess from Multiplicity and Me for the strength and hope that your honesty has given me. I am particularly grateful to Debbie Corso (Debbie De-Marco Bennett) whose blog and YouTube channel, Healing From BPD, made me feel seen when I felt invisible. In the first few years after I was diagnosed, I spent hours watching your videos sobbing with relief that somebody understood. There are countless, often anonymous, others I would like to thank for sharing personal experiences in various media. Every story that resonated with me made me feel less of an alien and more part of a community.

To Aya, my life-affirming dialectical behaviour therapist who worked with me for two momentous years. I didn't think anyone could understand the intensity of my emotions or convince me that I deserved self-compassion, but then (thank goodness!) I met you. Many mental health professionals could learn from your sense of justice, warmth and humour. You never once made me feel lesser for having a mental health condition because you treated me as an equal. Thank you for showing me how to have a calmer and happier life. I hope that I can pass on some of what you taught me in this book. Furthermore, I am indebted to Dr Marsha M. Linehan and her colleagues for creating DBT in the first place. I know it is not the only therapy for people who struggle to manage intense emotions, feel suicidal, and self-harm, but it has helped so many to survive immense pain and live more contented lives. I am ever grateful for Dr Marsha M. Linehan's book *DBT Skills Training Handouts and Worksheets* which has helped me hugely in writing this book, as well as in my life generally.

Thank you, Dr Maria P., my NHS consultant psychiatrist for several years, for seeing me for who I am and understanding how hard it is to live in the world right now with a diagnosis of borderline personality disorder. To the brilliant mental health nurse who helped me consider my sensitivity as a strength when shame almost swallowed me. I don't know your name, but I have never forgotten you. Thank you, Laura Robson Brown, my mentor during 2020, for helping me to reflect on all the threads in my life and how to hold onto them all. Thank you Folashade for working with me on confidence and trusting in myself whilst editing this book and processing a gigantic loss. To each and every Samaritan who listened to me crying down the phone until I could fall asleep or face the day – thank you.

Thank you to my friend Rosie MacPherson, for giving me confidence not only as a writer, but as a woman too. Thank you to my friend Louisa for introducing me to spoken word events when I needed their magic most. I am indebted to the poets, organizers and audiences of the London spoken word community for celebrating people who have previously been silenced. In front of your mics I felt like I was finally coming up for air.

Thank you especially to my one-in-a-million friend Astrid for your advice during the early days of this book, not to mention our precious friendship. Thank you to my wonderful friend Frances, (who gave me the orchid that inspired my blog's initial name) for friendship of the finest kind. Thank you to my generous friend Dr Sabina Dosani for being my anchor throughout the first COVID-19 lockdown when I wrote the first and second drafts of this book. I would also like to thank my teachers and fellow students from the Medical Humanities MSc at King's College London and the community of encouraging, like-minded friends I made there. Researching topics such as zines about self-harm, graphic narratives depicting childhood trauma and informally published artworks and texts about emotional distress was incredibly formative for me. Likewise, I am thankful to the Wellcome Collection library and its staff.

Eternal thanks to my extraordinary friend Dr Kathryn Watson who some readers will know from My Illustrated Mind. Since we met in cyberspace many moons ago, the unique connection and exceptional friendship we share has made my life immeasurably richer. Just by being yourself, you have given me so much. From the deepest depths of my heart, I want to thank my mum and dad. I would be hard pushed to find people as generous, loving or endlessly kind as you both. It is thanks to you that I, alongside my amazing sisters, have been able to embrace so many opportunities to learn, create, live a full life and, ultimately, become the person I am today. Finally, and most fundamentally, a whole ocean of thanks to my beloved partner, Maciek. The humour and happiness you have brought to my life makes me feel like the luckiest woman in the world. I can't thank you enough for your qualities, your way of thinking and, of course, your love.

talking about BPD

A Stigma-Free Guide to Living a Calmer, Happier Life with Borderline Personality Disorder

rosie cappuccino
foreword by kimberley wilson

Audiobook

Available for download from the JKP Library: https://library.jkp.com

ISBN 978 1 52937 104 8